W9-DBW-521

Careers
in Focus

Computers

Ferguson Publishing Company
Chicago, Illinois

Copyright © 1999 Ferguson Publishing Company
ISBN 0-89434-289-4

Library of Congress Cataloging-in-Publication Data

Careers in focus.   Computers.—2nd ed.
      p.   cm.
    Summary: Defines the top twenty-one careers in the computer field in
terms of the nature of the work, educational or training requirements, ways
to get started, advancement possibilities, salary figures, employment outlook,
conditions of work, and sources of more information.
    ISBN 0-89434-289-4
      1. Computer science—Vocational guidance. [1. Computer science—
Vocational guidance. 2. Vocational guidance.] I. Title: Computers.
QA76.25.C295   1999
004'.023—dc21   97-44045
                                                      CIP

Printed in the United States of America

Cover photo courtesy Tom Raymond/Tony Stone Images

Published and distributed by
Ferguson Publishing Company
200 West Jackson Boulevard
Chicago, Illinois 60606
312-692-1000

Y – 2

Table of Contents

Introduction

Computers can be divided into three broad categories—hardware, software, and the Internet. *Hardware* refers to the physical equipment of a computer, such as systems boards, memory chips, and microprocessors. *Software* includes the programs that tell the hardware exactly what to do and how to do it. Software is stored as digital impulses on magnetic disks. *The Internet* is composed of numerous global networks of computers that are connected to each other.

Computers have become increasingly important to business, government, and individuals over the past two decades—and the role they play is expected to keep increasing for the foreseeable future. As computers become integrated into more and more aspects of everyone's daily life, the need for professionals to design, operate, and repair them has grown, too.

Employment for computer professionals is expected to increase much faster than average as technology becomes more sophisticated and organizations continue to adopt and integrate these technologies, making for plentiful job openings. Falling prices of computer hardware and software should continue to induce more businesses to expand computerized operations and integrate new technologies. To maintain a competitive edge and operate more cost-effectively, firms will continue to demand computer professionals who are knowledgeable about the latest technologies and are able to apply them to the needs of business.

As for the Internet, the expanding integration of Internet technologies has resulted in a rising demand for a variety of skilled professionals who can develop and support Internet, Intranet, and World Wide Web applications. Growth in these areas is also expected to create demand for computer scientists, engineers, and systems analysts who are knowledgeable about networks, data, and communications security.

Employment opportunities in the computer industry are numerous and varied. Flexibility is also key because as the industry shifts into new, unexplored areas, computer professionals have to shift as well. In addition, many computer professionals use certain jobs as springboards to other higher level jobs. For example, few professionals want to work in technical support longterm, but many start there to have a foot in the door for when internal positions open up. If people are so specialized that such professional moving around is impossible, they might have difficulties in the future.

Each article in this book discusses a particular computer occupation in detail. The information comes from Ferguson's *Encyclopedia of Careers and Vocational Guidance*. The History section describes the history of the particular job as it relates to the overall development of its industry or field. The Job describes the primary and secondary duties of the job. Requirements discusses high school and postsecondary education and training requirements, any certification or licensing necessary, and any other personal requirements for success in the job. Exploring offers suggestions on how to gain some experience in or knowledge of the particular job before making a firm educational and financial commitment. The focus is on what can be done while still in high school (or in the early years of college) to gain a better understanding of the job. The Employers section gives an overview of typical places of employment for the job. Starting Out discusses the best ways to land that first job, be it through the college placement office, newspaper ads, or personal contact. The Advancement section describes what kind of career path to expect from the job and how to get there. Earnings lists salary ranges and describes the typical fringe benefits. The Work Environment section describes the typical surroundings and conditions of employment—whether indoors or outdoors, noisy or quiet, social or independent, and so on. Also discussed are typical hours worked, any seasonal fluctuations, and the stresses and strains of the job. The Outlook section summarizes the job in terms of the general economy and industry projections. For the most part, Outlook information is obtained from the Bureau of Labor Statistics and is supplemented by information taken from professional associations. Job growth terms follow those used in the *Occupational Outlook Handbook:* Growth described as "much faster than the average" means an increase of 36 percent or more. Growth described as "faster than the average" means an increase of 21 to 35 percent. Growth described as "about as fast as the average" means an increase of 10 to 20 percent. Growth described as "little change or more slowly than the average" means an increase of 0 to 9 percent. "Decline" means a decrease of 1 percent or more.

Each article ends with For More Information, which lists organizations that can provide career information on training, education, internships, scholarships, and job placement.

Computer and Electronics Sales Representatives

Business Computer science Speech	School Subjects
Communication/ideas Technical/scientific	Personal Skills
Primarily indoors Primarily multiple locations	Work Environment
Bachelor's degree	Minimum Education Level
$11,000 to $52,000 to $100,000+	Salary Range
None available	Certification or Licensing
About as fast as the average	Outlook

Overview

Computer and electronics sales representatives sell hardware, software, peripheral computer equipment, and electronics equipment to customers and businesses of all sizes. Sometimes they follow up sales with installation of systems, maintenance, or training of the client's staff. They are employed in all aspects of business. Sales representatives whowork for retail stores deal with consumers. Representatives whospecialize in a particular piece of hardware, certain software program, or electronic component may do business with banks, insurance companies, or accounting firms, among others.

History

The first major advances in modern computer technology were made during World War II. After the war, people thought that computers were too big (they easily filled entire warehouses) to ever be used for anything other than government projects, such as their use in compiling the 1950 census.

The introduction of semiconductors to computer technology made smaller and less expensive computers possible. The semiconductors replaced the bigger, slower vacuum tubes of the first computers. These changes made it easier for businesses to adapt computers to their needs, which they began doing as early as 1954. Within 30 years, computers revolutionized the way people work, play, and even shop. Few occupations have remained untouched by this technological revolution. Consequently, computers are found in businesses, government offices, hospitals, schools, science labs, and homes. Clearly, there is a huge market for the sale of computers and peripheral equipment. There is an important need today for knowledgeable sales representatives to serve both the retail public and to advise corporations and large organizations on their computer and electronics purchases.

The Job

The first step in the selling process, no matter the sales environment—retail or corporate—is client consultation. Sales representatives determine the client's current technological needs, as well as those of the future. During consultation, reps explain the technology's value and how well it will perform. Often, customers do not have expertise in computer or electronics technology, so the rep must explain and translate complicated computer tech-talk, as well as answer numerous questions. In retail computer sales, the customer decides what system, peripheral, or software to purchase and then takes it home or arranges for its delivery.

In the corporate sales environment, client consultations usually take longer, often entailing numerous trips to the client's office or place of business. Ron Corrales, an Account Support Manager for Anderson Consulting, acknowledges client consultation is the crucial first step in the sales process. After the client's business is researched and its needs assessed, possible solutions are outlined in the form of a written or oral presentation. "I was really nervous the first few times I gave a presentation," recalls Ron. "After all, these were CEOs and CFOs of Fortune 500 companies!" The talent for public speaking and technical writing frequently comes into play. Sales representatives must be able to effectively and clearly present the product and its capabilities, often in layperson's terms. After perfecting his communication skills, Ron now thinks of client presentations as "just part of the job."

Anderson Consulting (AC) is the largest IT (Information Technology) consulting firm in the world. It provides proprietary software used by businesses worldwide. AC's programs are tools tailor-made to fit the needs of each company and its specific routines, such as accounting, customer billing, inventory control, and marketing. AC's client list includes the grocery store chain Kroger's, Harley Davidson, and the U.S. government.

After the presentation, if all goes well, Ron helps draft the contract. Every aspect of the agreement is outlined and specified—the type of software and length of contract, including services, training, or maintenance. The deal is considered "done" once the AC partners and the client CEOs sign, and of course, the fees are paid. Once the companies receive their software, it is installed and glitches, if any, are resolved. Many times, company employees are trained by AC consultants on how to use the software to its fullest capability. Usually, a one year maintenance contract is provided to the client.

To stay abreast of technological advances, sales representatives must attend training sessions or continuing education classes. It also helps to know the essence of each client's field and the nature of their work. Weekly departmental meetings are necessary to know of any developments or projects within the department, or AC as a whole. A big part of Ron's job is managing his territory, making client calls or visits when necessary. A chunk of his work day is devoted to "putting out potential client 'fires.'"

Requirements

High School

Classes in speech and writing will help you learn how to communicate your product to large groups of people. Computer science and electronics classes will give you a basic overview of the field. General business and math classes will also be helpful.

Postsecondary Training

Though a small number of computer sales positions may be filled by high school graduates, those jobs are scarce. Most large companies prefer a bachelor's or advanced degree in computer science or related background, marketing, or business.

Prepare yourself for a career in this field by developing your computer knowledge—take computer and math classes as well as business classes to help develop a sound business sense. Since sales representatives are often required to meet with clients and make sales presentations, excellent communications skills are a must. Hone yours by taking English and speech classes.

In this particular field of sales, extensive computer knowledge is just as important as business savvy. Most computer sales representatives pursue computer science courses concurrently with their business classes. For computer sales representatives specializing in a specific industry, say health care or banking, training in the basics and current issues of that field is needed. Such training can be obtained through special work training seminars, adult education classes, or courses at a technical school. Many companies require their sales staff to complete a training program where they'll learn the technologies and work tools needed for the job. (This is where you'll pick up the techno-speak for your specific field.)

Ron holds a Master of Information Science degree. One of the college classes that has helped him the most in his career is "technical writing and communication—it helps to be able to explain complicated and technical material in layperson terms."

Other Requirements

Equally important as formal education and computer and electronics knowledge is having a "sales" personality. Sales representatives must be confident and knowledgeable about themselves as well as the product they are selling. They should have strong interpersonal skills and enjoy dealing with all types of people—from families buying their first PCs, to CEOs of Fortune 500 companies. "People in this business are well-rounded and enjoy technology," Ron adds, "but, to do well, they need to be competitively hungry, and like to talk—a lot!"

Employers

Employment opportunities for this field exist nationwide. What are your priorities? Do you want to work for an industry giant? IBM? Microsoft? Motorola? You may be enticed with attractive perks—stock options, big travel expense account, graduate school tuition, among other benefits. Note, however, that these are huge corporations; you'll really have to be something special if you want to stand apart from the other applicants. Getting hired is tough, too. Microsoft, for example, receives thousands of resumes weekly.

Middle-size and small companies usually require their employees to don several hats. That means sales representatives may be responsible for their entire presentations, including product and client research as well as maintenance and service. It may sound like much work, and for some tasks you may feel over qualified. The rewards include being part of the ground team when your company takes off. If it doesn't, you can always chalk it up to good experience.

Starting Out

That Ron had two job offers by graduation is not uncommon, especially for students with computer-related majors. Many top companies aggressively recruit on campus, often enticing soon-to-be grads with signing bonuses or other incentives at school-sponsored job fairs.

Other avenues to try when conducting your job search include the newspaper job ads and trade papers. Try the Internet, too. Many companies maintain Web sites where they post employment opportunities and receive online resumes and applications. Your school's job placement center is a great place to start your job search. Not only will the counselors have information on jobs not advertised in the paper, but they can also provide tips on resume writing and interviewing techniques.

Advancement

With a good work record, a computer or electronics sales representative may be offered a position in management. A manager is responsible for supervising the sales for a given retail store, sales territory, or corporate branch. A management position comes not only with a higher salary but with a higher level of responsibility as well. An effective manager should be well versed in the company's products and sales techniques and be able to keep a sales group working at top capacity. Those already at the management level may decide to transfer to the marketing side of the business. Positions in marketing may involve planning the marketing strategy for a new computer or electronics product and coordinating sales campaigns and product distribution.

Earnings

There is great variance regarding annual salaries for this field. Electronics and computer sales representatives working in retail are paid an hourly wage—usually minimum wage, $5.15 an hour—supplemented with commissions based on a percentage of sales made that day or week. Earnings will also depend upon the size and type of employer. Electronics sales representatives earned an average of $423 a week in 1996, as listed in the *1998-99 Occupational Outlook Handbook*.

Computer sales representatives specializing in corporate sales of hardware or software tend to earn quite a bit more. First, corporate sales people usually hold a college degree. They also deal with larger sales packages that mean larger commissions. According to a recent WetFeet.com Industry study, sales associates specializing in hardware components averaged from $30,000 to $40,000 base salary; commissions raised the final averages to between $45,000 and $60,000 a year. Salaries are dependent on the product sold—PCs, mainframes, peripherals—and the market served.

A 1998 international sales and marketing salary survey conducted by Sales & Marketing Executives International pegged annual salaries a bit higher. Experienced account representatives in the computer/information field earned an annual salary of about $52,000; sales managers earned about $75,000; and marketing managers earned $104,125. (Year-end bonuses are often given to employees, greatly enhancing their final yearly salary.)

Most computer sales representatives are offered benefit packages including health and life insurance, paid holidays and vacations, continuing education and training, and volume bonuses or stock options.

Work Environment

Retail sales representatives work in a retail environment. A 40-hour work-week is typical, though longer hours may be necessary during busy shopping seasons. Whether or not the sales representative is compensated during these extended hours varies from store to store. However, increased work times usually means increased sales volume, which in the end, translates to more commissions. Retail representatives must be prepared to deal with a large volume of customers with varying levels of technical knowledge, all with many questions. It is necessary to treat customers with respect and patience, regardless of the size of the sale—or if a sale is made at all.

Corporate sales representatives, like Ron, work in a professional office environment. Work is conducted at the home office as well as in the field when making sales calls. Work schedules vary depending on the size of territory and number of clients. A 40-hour workweek is the exception, rather than the rule. "I average about 60+ hours a week," says Ron. "My hours are flexible, but with a lot of weekend work and travel."

Outlook

Employment opportunities should remain healthy for computer and electronics-related sales careers through the year 2006. As computer companies continue to price their products competitively, more and more people will be able to afford new home computer systems or to upgrade existing ones with the latest hardware, software, and peripherals. Increased retail sales will warrant competent and knowledgeable sales representatives. Many jobs exist at retail giants (Best Buy and Office Depot, known for office-related supplies and equipment, are two examples) that provide consumers with good price packages as well as optional services, such as installation and maintenance.

Employment opportunities can also be found with computer specialty stores or consulting companies that deal directly with businesses and their corporate computer and application needs. Computers have become an almost indispensable tool for running a successful business—be it an accounting firm, public relations company, or a multi-physician medical practice. As long as this trend continues, knowledgeable sales representatives will be needed to bring the latest technological advances in hardware and software to the consumer and corporate levels.

For More Information

For industry or membership information, contact:

National Association of Retail Dealers of America
10 East 22nd Street
Lombard, IL 60148-4915
Tel: 630-953-8950
Email: nardahdq@aol.com
Web: http://www.Narda.com

Contact ACM for information on internships, student membership, and the ACM student magazine, Crossroads. *ACM also offers a student Web site at http://www.acm.org/membership/student/.*

Association for Computing Machinery
1515 Broadway
New York, NY 10036-5701
Tel: 212-869-7440
Email: SIGS@acm.org
Web: http://www.acm.org

The Electronics Representatives Association is the trade organization of professional sales and marketing companies that specialize in multiple-line selling of computers, software, and other electronic products. For industry and membership information, or for a copy of The Representor, *a quarterly trade magazine, contact:*

The Electronics Representatives Association
444 North Michigan Avenue, Suite 1960
Chicago, IL 60611
Tel: 312-527-3050
Email: info@era.org
Web: http://www.era.org

Computer and Office Machine Service Technicians

School Subjects
Computer science
Technical/shop

Personal Skills
Mechanical/manipulative
Technical/scientific

Work Environment
Primarily indoors
Primarily multiple locations

Minimum Education Level
Bachelor's degree

Salary Range
$15,000 to $30,264 to $40,000

Certification or Licensing
Required by all states

Outlook
Much faster than the average

Overview

Computer and office machine service technicians install, calibrate, maintain, troubleshoot, and repair equipment such as computers and their peripherals, office equipment, and specialized electronic equipment used in many factories, hospitals, airplanes, and numerous other businesses. Potential employers include computer companies and large corporations that need staff devoted to repairing and maintaining their equipment. Many service technicians are employed by companies that contract their services to other businesses. According to the *Occupational Outlook Handbook,* of the 396,000 service technicians employed in the United States in 1996, 141,000 specialized in computer repair and maintenance; the remaining technicians specialized in office machinery, communications equipment, telephone repair, or home entertainment electronics.

History

When computers were first introduced to the business world, businesses found their size to be cumbersome and their capabilities limited. Today, technological advances have made computers smaller, yet more powerful in their speed and capabilities. As more businesses rely on computers and other office machines to help manage daily activities, access information, and link offices and resources, the need for experienced professionals to operate and service these machines will increase. Service technicians are employed by corporations, hospitals, and the government. They may be part of a permanent staff, or they may be contracted to work for other businesses.

The Job

L3 Communications manufactures computer systems for a diverse group of clients, such as Shell Oil, United Airlines, and the Chicago Board of Trade. Besides computer systems, they also offer services such as equipment maintenance contracts and customer training. Joey Arca, a service technician for L3 Communications, loves the challenge and diversity of his job. He and other members of the staff are responsible for the installation of computer mainframes and systems as well as for training employees on the equipment. A large part of their work is the maintenance, diagnostic, and repair of computer equipment. Since the clients are located throughout the United States, Joey must often travel to different cities in his assigned district. He also presents company products and services to potential clients and bids for maintenance contracts.

"I don't always have to be at the office—which gives me a lot of freedom," says Joey. "Sometimes I call in from my home and get my scheduled appointments for the day." The freedom of not being deskbound does have its downside. "One of the most difficult parts of the job is not knowing when a computer will fail. I carry a pager 24/7, and if I get called, I'm bound to a two-hour response time."

Many times work is scheduled before or after regular working hours, or on the weekend since it's important to have the least amount of workday disruption. Joey is successful in his job because he keeps on top of constantly changing technology by attending continuing education classes and training seminars. He is also well versed in both hardware and software, especially systems software.

When asked what kind of people are best suited for this line of work, Joey replied, "task oriented, quantitatively smart, organized, and personable. Also, they need the ability to convey technical terms in writing and orally."

Requirements

High School

Traditional high school courses such as mathematics, physical sciences, and other laboratory-based sciences can provide a strong foundation for understanding basic mechanical and electronics principles. English and speech classes can help boost your written and verbal communication skills.

Postsecondary Training

A high school diploma is the minimum requirement for pursuing a career in this field, though many computer service technicians have advanced degrees. Joey, for example, holds a bachelor of science degree in electrical engineering. He credits specialized classes, such as Voice and Data Communications, Microprocessor Controls, and Digital Circuits, with giving him a good base for his current work environment.

Certification or Licensing

Certification is required by most employers, though standards vary depending on the company. However, it is considered by many as a measure of industry knowledge. Certification can also give you a competitive edge when interviewing for a new job or negotiating for a higher salary.

A variety of certification programs are available from the International Society of Certified Electronics Technicians and the Institute for Certification of Computing Professional, among other organizations. After the successful completion of study and examination, you may be certified in fields such as computer, industrial, and electronic equipment. Continuing education credits are required for recertification, usually every two to four years. Joey is certified as a computer technician by the Association of Energy Engineers and the Electronics Technicians Association and Satellite Dealers Association.

Other Requirements

A strong technical background, an aptitude for learning about new technologies, good communication skills, and superior manual dexterity will help you succeed in this industry. You'll also need to be motivated to keep up with modern computer and office machine technology. Machines rapidly become obsolete, and so does the service technician's training. When new equipment is installed, service technicians must demonstrate the intellectual agility to learn how to handle problems that might arise.

Employers

Though work opportunities for service technicians are available nationwide, many jobs are located in large cities where computer companies and larger corporations are based. Joey's employer, like many other service contractors, is headquartered in Anaheim, California, but maintains satellite offices throughout the United States.

Starting Out

If your school offers placement services, then use them. Many times, school placement and counseling centers are privy to job openings that are filled without being advertised in the newspaper. Make sure your counselors know of your important preferences—location, specialization, and other requirements—so they can best match you to an employer. Don't forget to supply them with an updated resume.

There are also other avenues to take when searching for a job in this industry. Many jobs are advertised in the jobs section of your local newspaper. Look under "Computers" or "Electronics." Also, inquire directly with the personnel departments of companies that appeal to you and fill out applications. Trade association Web sites are good sources of job leads; many will post employment opportunities as well as allow you to post your resume.

Advancement

Due to the growth of computer products and their influence over the business world, this industry offers a variety of advancement opportunities. Service technicians usually start by working on relatively simple maintenance and repair tasks. Over time, they start working on more complicated projects.

Experienced service technicians may advance to positions of increased responsibility, such as crew supervisor or department manager. Another advancement route is to become a sales representative for a computer manufacturing company. Technicians develop hands-on knowledge of particular machines and are thus often in the best position to advise potential buyers about important purchasing decisions. Some entrepreneurial-minded servicers might open their own repair businesses, which can be risky but can also provide many rewards. Unless they fill a certain market niche, technicians usually find it necessary to service a wide range of computers and office machines.

Earnings

According to the *Occupational Outlook Handbook,* in 1996, service technicians specializing in communications and industrial electronic equipment earned an average annual salary of $31,304; computer equipment service technicians earned an average of $30,264 a year. Technicians with extensive work experience and certification earn more.

Standard work benefits include health and life insurance, paid vacation and sick time, and retirement plans. Most technicians are given travel stipends; some receive company cars.

Work Environment

"I like the freedom of not working in a (typical) office environment and the short workweeks," says Joey. Most service technicians, however, have unpredictable work schedules. Some weeks are quiet and may warrant fewer work hours. However, during a major computer problem, or worse yet, a breakdown, technicians are required to work around the clock to fix the problem as quickly as possible. Technicians spend considerable time on call and must carry a pager in case of work emergencies.

Travel is an integral part of the job for many service technicians, many times amounting to 80 percent of the job time. Joey has even traveled to the Philippines where he worked on the Tomahawk Missile project at Clark Air Force Base. Since he is originally from the Philippines, he was able to combine work with a visit with friends and family.

Outlook

According to the *Occupational Outlook Handbook,* employment opportunities for service technicians working with computer and office equipment are expected to grow much faster than the average—about 37 percent faster than the average for all other occupations. Demand for service technicians specializing in commercial and industrial electronic equipment is expected to grow about 12 percent. As corporations, governments, hospitals, and universities worldwide continue their reliance on computers to help manage their daily business, demand for qualified, skilled technicians will increase.

Modern office equipment is better designed and can run longer without needing maintenance or repair. As a result, demand for service technicians specializing in office equipment repair is expected to grow only as fast as the average.

For More Information

For certification information, contact:

Institute for Certification of Computing Professionals
2200 East Devon Avenue, Suite 247
Des Plaines, IL 60018-4503
Tel: 847-299-4227
Web: http://www.iccp.org

For industry information or details on their certification program, contact:

International Society of Certified Electronics Technicians
2708 West Berry Street
Fort Worth, TX 76109-2356
Tel: 817-921-9101
Web: http://www.iscet.org

Contact ACM for information on internships, student membership, and the ACM magazine, Crossroads. ACM also offers a student Web site at http://www.acm.org/membership/student/:

Association for Computing Machinery
1515 Broadway, 17th Floor
New York, NY 10036-5701
Tel: 212-869-7440
Email: SIGS@acm.org
Web: http://www.acm.org

For certification, career, and placement information, contact:

Electronics Technicians Association and Satellite Dealers Association
602 North Jackson
Greencastle, IN 46135
Tel: 765-653-4301
Web: http://www.eta-sda.com

Computer and Video Game Designers

Overview

In the sector of the multibillion-dollar computer industry known as interactive entertainment and recreational computing, *computer and video game designers* create and document the ideas and interactivity for games played on various platforms, or media, such as video consoles and computers, and through online Internet subscriptions. They generate ideas for new game concepts, including sound effects, characters, story lines, and graphics.

Because the industry is fairly new, it is difficult to estimate how many people work as game designers. Around 90,000 people work within the video game industry as a whole. Designers work for companies that make the games or create the games on their own and sell their ideas and programs to companies that produce them.

History

Computer and video game designers are a relatively new breed. The industry didn't begin to develop until the 1960s and 1970s, when computer programmers at some large universities, big companies, and government labs began designing games on mainframe computers. Steve Russell was perhaps the first video game designer—in 1962, when he was in college, he made up a simple game called Spacewar. Graphics of space ships flew through a starry sky on the video screen; the object of the game was to shoot down enemy ships. Nolan Bushnell, another early designer, played Spacewar in college. In 1972, he put the first video game in an arcade; it was a game very much like Spacewar, and he called it Computer Space. However, many users found the game difficult to play, so it wasn't a success.

Bruce Artwick published the first of many versions of Flight Simulator, and Bushnell later created Pong, a game that required the players to paddle electronic ping-pong balls back and forth across the video screen. Pong was a big hit, and players spent thousands of quarters in arcade machines all over the country playing it. Bushnell's company, Atari, had to hire more and more designers every week. These designers included Steve Jobs, Alan Kay, and Chris Crawford. Early designers made games with text-based descriptions (that is, no graphics) of scenes and actions with interactivity done through a computer keyboard. Games called Adventure, Star Trek, and Flight Simulator were among the first that designers created. They used simple commands like "look at building" and "move west." Most games were designed for video machines; not until the later 1970s did specially equipped TVs and early personal computers (PCs) begin appearing.

In the late 1970s and early 1980s, designers working for Atari and Intellivision made games for home video systems, PCs, and video arcades. Many of these new games had graphics, sound, text, and animation. Designers of games like Pac-Man, Donkey Kong, and Space Invaders were successful and popular. They also started to make role-playing games like the famous Dungeons and Dragons. Richard Garriott created Ultima, another major role-playing game. Games began to feature the names and photos of their programmers on the packaging, giving credit to individual designers.

Workers at Electronic Arts began to focus on making games for PCs to take advantage of technology that included the computer keyboard, more memory, and 5-1/4-inch floppy disks. They created games like Carmen Sandiego and M.U.L.E. In the mid to late 1980s, new technology included 3.5-inch floppies, sound cards, and larger memory. Designers also had to create games that would work on more than just one platform—PCs, Apple computers, and 64-bit video game machines.

In the 1990s, Electronic Arts started to hire teams of designers instead of "lone wolf" individuals (those who design games from start to finish independently). Larger teams were needed because games got more complex; design teams would include not only programmers but also artists, musicians, writers, and animators. Designers made such breakthroughs as using more entertaining graphics, creating more depth in role-playing games, using virtual reality in sports games, and using more visual realism in racing games and flight simulators. This new breed of designers created games using techniques such as Assembly, C, and HyperCard. By 1994, designers began to use CD-ROM technology to its fullest. In only a few months, Doom was a hit—designers of this game gave players the chance to alter it themselves at various levels, including choices of weapons and enemies. Doom still has fans worldwide.

The success of *shareware* (software that is given away to attract users to want to buy more complete software) has influenced the return of smaller groups of designers. Even the lone wolf is coming back, using shareware and better authoring tools such as sound libraries and complex multimedia development environments. Some designers are finding that they work best on their own or in small teams.

What's on the horizon for game designers? More multiplayer games (like Doom); virtual reality; improved technology in coprocessors, chips, hardware, and sound fonts; and "persistent worlds," where online games are influenced by and evolve from players' actions. These new types of games require that designers know more and more complex code so that games can "react" to their multiple players.

The Job

Designing games involves programming code as well as creating stories, graphics, and sound effects. It is a very creative process, requiring imagination and computer and communication skills to develop games that are interactive and entertaining. As mentioned earlier, some game designers work on their own and try to sell their designs to companies that produce and distribute games; others are employees of companies like Electronic Arts, Broderbund, and many others. Whether you work alone or for a company, your aim is to create games that get players involved. Game players want to have fun, they want to be challenged; sometimes they want to learn something along the way.

Each game must have a storyline as well as graphics and sound that will entertain and engage the players. *Storylines* are situations that the players will find themselves in and make decisions about. Designers develop a plan for combining the story or concept, music or other sound effects, and graphics. They design rules to make it fun, challenging, or educational, and they create characters for the stories or circumstances, worlds in which these characters live, and problems or situations these characters will face.

One of the first steps is to identify the audience that will be playing the game. How old are the players? What kinds of things are they interested in? What kind of game will it be: action? adventure? "edutainment"? role-playing? sports? And for which platform will the game be used: video (e.g., Nintendo Ultra 64), computer (e.g., Macintosh with System 8.5), or online (Internet via subscription)?

The next steps are to create a design proposal, a preliminary design, and a final game design. The proposal is a brief summary of what the game involves. The preliminary design goes much further, outlining in more detail what the concept is (the story of the game); how the players get involved; what sound effects, graphics, and other elements will be included (what will the screen look like? what kind of sound effects should the player hear?); and what productivity tools (such as word processors, database programs, spreadsheet programs, flowcharting programs, and prototyping programs) you intend to use to create these elements. Independent designers submit a product idea and design proposal to a publisher along with a cover letter and resume. Employees work as part of a team to create the proposal and design. Teamwork might include brainstorming sessions to come up with ideas as well as involvement in market research (surveying the players who will be interested in the game).

The final game design details the basic idea, the plot, and every section of the game, including the start-up process, all the scenes (or other comparable elements, such as innings for baseball games and maps for edutainment games), and all the universal elements (rules for scoring, names of characters, and sound effects that occur every time something specific happens). The story, characters, worlds, and maps are documented. The game design also includes details of the logic of the game, its algorithms (the step-by-step procedures for solving the problems the players will encounter), and its rules; the methods the player will use to load the game, start it up, score, win, lose, save, stop, and play again; the graphic design, including storyboards and sample art; the audio design. The designer might also include marketing ideas and proposed follow-up games.

Designers interact with other workers and technologists involved in the game design project, including programmers, audio engineers, artists, and even asset managers, who coordinate the collecting, engineering, and distribution of physical assets to the production team (the people who will actually produce the physical CD-ROM or videocassette).

Designers need to understand games and their various forms, think up new ideas, and experiment with and evaluate new designs. They assemble the separate elements (text, art, sound, video) of a game into a complete, interactive form, following through with careful planning and preparation (such as sketching out scripts, storyboards, and design documents). They write an implementation plan and guidelines (how will you manage the process? how much will it cost to design the game? how long will the guidelines be—five pages? three hundred?). Finally, they amend designs at every stage, solving problems and answering questions.

Computer and video game designers often keep scrapbooks, notes, and journals of interesting ideas and other bits of information. They collect potential game material and even catalog ideas, videos, movies, pictures, stories, character descriptions, music clips, sound effects, animation sequences, and interface techniques. The average time it takes to design a game, including all the elements and stages just described, can be from about 6 to 18 months.

Requirements

High School

If you like to play Doom, Harpoon, or Ultima, you're already familiar with games. You will also need to learn a programming language like C++ or Java, and you'll need a good working knowledge of the hardware platform for which you plan to develop your games (video, computer, online). In high school learn as much as you can about computers: how they work, what kinds there are, how to program them, and any languages available to you. You should also take physics, chemistry, and computer science. Since designers are creative, take courses such as art, literature, and music as well.

Postsecondary Training

Although strictly speaking you don't have to have a college degree to be a game designer, more companies are looking for creative people who also have degrees. Having one represents that you've been actively involved in intense, creative work; that you can work with others and follow through on assignments; and of course that you've learned what there is to know about programming, computer architecture (including input devices, processing devices, memory and storage devices, and output devices), and software engineering. Employers want to know that you've had some practical experience in design.

Only one accredited school grants a degree in game design: DigiPen, in Redmond, Washington. Also, the University of North Texas has a Laboratory for Recreational Computing (LARC), which offers a senior elective course called Computer Game Design and Programming. The college courses you should take include: programming (including assembly level), computer architecture, software engineering, computer graphics, data structures, algorithms, communications networks, artificial intelligence (AI) and expert systems, interface systems, mathematics, and physics.

According to Professor Ian Parberry of LARC, the quality of your education depends a lot on your. "You must take control of your education, seek out the best professors, and go beyond the material presented in class. . . . What you have a right to expect from an undergraduate computer science degree is a grasp of the fundamental concepts of computer science and enough practical skills to be able to grow, learn, and thrive in any computational environment, be it computer games or otherwise."

Other Requirements

One major requirement for game design is that you must love to play computer games. You need to continually keep up with technology, which changes fast. Although you might not always use them, you need to have a variety of skills, such as writing stories, programming, and designing sound effects.

You must have vision and the ability to identify your players and anticipate their every move in your game. You'll also have to be able to communicate well with programmers, writers, artists, musicians, electronics engineers, production workers, and others.

You must have the endurance to see a project through from beginning to end and also be able to recognize when a design should be scrapped.

Exploring

One of the best ways to learn about game design is to try to develop copies of easy games, like Pong and Pac-Man, or try to change a game that has an editor. (Games like Klik & Play, Empire, and Doom allow players to modify them to create new circumstances.)

For high school students interested in finding out more about how video games and animations are produced, the DigiPen Institute of Technology offers a summer workshop. Two-week courses are offered during July and August, providing hands-on experience and advice on courses to take in high school to prepare yourself for postsecondary training.

Writing your own stories, puzzles, and games helps develop storytelling and problem-solving skills. Magazines like *Computer Graphics World* (http://www.cgw.com) and *Game Developer* (http://www.gdmag.com) have articles about digital video and high-end imaging, and other technical and design information.

Employers

Software publishers (like Electronic Arts and Activision) are found throughout the country, though most are located in California, New York, Washington, and Illinois. Electronic Arts is the largest independent publisher of interactive entertainment. It includes several development studios and is known worldwide. Big media companies, such as Disney, have also opened interactive entertainment departments. Jobs should be available at these companies as well as with online services and interactive networks, which are growing rapidly.

Some companies are involved in producing games only for video; others produce only for computers; others make games for various platforms. For example, Nintendo produces software only for video consoles; it makes different kinds of products but focuses on arcade, sports, and role-playing games. Byron Preiss Multimedia produces only PC-based adventure and multimedia games. Electronic Arts runs the gamut—video, PC, and Internet, producing almost every genre, from sports to adventure to edutainment.

Starting Out

There are a couple of ways to begin earning money as a game designer: independently or as an employee of a company. It is more realistic to get any creative job you can in the industry (for example, as an artist, a play tester, a programmer, or a writer) and learn as you go, developing your design skills as you work your way up to the level of designer.

Contact company Web sites and sites that advertise job openings, like Game Jobs at http://www.gamejobs.com, the WWW Employment Office at http://www.harbornet.com/biz/office/annex.html, and E-Span at http://www.espan.com.

In addition to a professional resume, it's a good idea to have your own Web site, where you can showcase your demos. Make sure you have designed at least one demo or have an impressive portfolio of design ideas and documents.

Other ways to find a job in the industry include going to job fairs (like the Computer Game Developers Conference), where you find recruiters looking for creative people to work at their companies, and checking in with CompuServe's game developers forum (GAMEDEV) and user groups, which often post jobs on the Internet.

Advancement

Just as with many other jobs, to have better opportunities to advance your position and possibly earn more money you have to keep up with technology. Be willing to constantly learn more about design, the industry, and even financial and legal matters involved in development.

Becoming and remaining great at your job may be a career-long endeavor or or just a stepping stone to another area of interactive entertainment. Some designers start out as artists, writers, or programmers and learn enough in these jobs to eventually design. For example, you may begin as a 3-D animation modeler and work on enough game life cycles to understand what it takes to be a game designer. You may decide to specialize in another area, such as sound effects or even budgeting.

Some designers aspire to management positions, like president or vice president of a software publisher. Others write for magazines and books, teach, or establish their own game companies.

Earnings

Most development companies spend up to two years designing a game even before any of the mechanics (like writing final code and drawing final graphics) begin; more complex games take even longer. Companies budget $1-3 million for developing just one game. If the game is a success, designers are often rewarded with bonuses. According to the *Game Developer's Marketplace*, game designers earn from $30,000 to $75,000 a year.

Earnings also depend on how much experience you have, where you live, possible bonuses and royalties (the percentage of profits you receive from each game that is sold), and the size of the company you work for.

Any major software publisher is likely to provide benefits such as medical insurance, paid vacations, and retirement plans. If you are self-employed you must provide your own benefits.

Work Environment

Computer and video game designers work in office settings, whether at a large company or a home studio. At some companies, artists and designers sometimes find themselves work 24 to 48 hours at a time, so the office areas are set up with sleeping couches and other areas where employees can relax. Because the game development industry is competitive, many designers are under a lot of pressure—from deadlines, design problems, and budget concerns.

Outlook

The computer and video game industry is growing quickly, with more and more companies hiring skilled people at many levels.

Estimates of the number of game designers working in the United States are not readily available, mainly because the industry is so young. *Game Developer's Marketplace* mentions that, according to the Interactive Digital Software Association, about 90,000 people work at all positions in the entertainment software field and that 50,000 people are employed at some level of the U.S. game development industry.

In any case, game development is popular—it is estimated that 15 million people in the United States have grown up playing computer and video games and that this number could go beyond 100 million by the year 2010. People in the industry expect more and more integration of interactive entertainment into mainstream society. Online development tools, like engines and graphic and sound libraries, as well as programming languages, like Java, will probably create opportunities for new types of products that can feature game components.

For More Information

CGDA aims to enhance the quality of computer games, interactive entertainment, and educational software; increase artistic and financial recognition for developers; and support the provision of professional education to members of the industry.

Computer Game Developers Association (CGDA)
Email: info@cgda.org
Web: http://www.cgda.org

The following institute is authorized by the Washington State Higher Education Coordinating Board to offer the world's first-ever bachelor of science degree in Real Time Interactive Simulation, dedicated to the programming of interactive computer and video games.

DigiPen Institute of Technology
5001 150th Avenue, NE
Redmond, WA 98052
Tel: 425-558-0299
Email: info@digipen.edu
Web: http://www.digipen.edu

This grassroots group provides designers with direct access to people and materials.

International Game Developers Network
1030 East El Camino Real, #210
Sunnyvale, CA 94087
Web: http://igdn.org

Computer Network Administrators

Computer science Mathematics	School Subjects
Helping/teaching Leadership/management Technical/scientific	Personal Skills
Primarily indoors Primarily one location	Work Environment
Bachelor's degree	Minimum Education Level
$46,200 to $57,700 to $71,700+	Salary Range
Recommended	Certification or Licensing
Faster than the average	Outlook

Overview

Computer network administrators, or *network specialists,* design, install, and support an organization's local area network (LAN), wide area network (WAN), network segment, or Internet system. They maintain network hardware and software, analyze problems, and monitor the network to ensure availability to system users. Administrators also might plan, coordinate, and implement network security measures, including firewalls.

History

The first major advances in modern computer technology were made during World War II. After the war, it was thought that the enormous size of computers, which easily took up the space of entire warehouses, would limit their use to huge government projects. For example, the 1950 census was computer processed.

The introduction of semiconductors to computer technology made possible smaller and less expensive computers. Businesses began adapting computers to their operations as early as 1954. Within 30 years, computers revolutionized the way people work, play, and shop. Today, computers are everywhere, from businesses of all kinds, to government agencies, charitable organizations, and private homes. Over the years, technology has continued to shrink computer size and increase computer speed at an unprecedented rate.

The first commercially used computers consisted of big mainframe computers located in a special computer rooms and several independent terminals around the office. Though efficient and effective, the mainframe had several problems. One problem was the update delay, or the time lapse, between when an employee input information and when that information became available to other employees. Though advances in hardware technology have begun addressing this and other problems of mainframes, many computer companies and businesses have turned to networking instead.

Computer networks do not rely on a mainframe system, but rather use a network server to centralize the processing capacity of several different computers and peripherals. In a network, terminals and other computers are linked directly to the server. This link provides other computer users access to the information instantaneously. The increased need for computer network administrators who are qualified to oversee network operations has paralleled the growth of computer networking.

The use of networks has grown rapidly as more companies move from mainframe computers to client-server networks or from paper-based systems to automated record-keeping using networked databases. The explosion of Internet technology has created a new area that also is in need of networking professionals.

The Job

Businesses use computer networks for several reasons. One important reason is that networks make it easy for many employees to share hardware and software as well as printers, faxes, and modems. For example, it would be very expensive to buy individual copies of word-processing programs for each employee in a company. By investing in a network version of the software that all employees can access, companies can often save a lot of money. Also, businesses that rely on databases for daily operations use networks to allow authorized personnel quick and easy access to the most updated version of the database.

Networks vary greatly in size; even just two computers connected together are considered a network. They can also be extremely large and complex, involving hundreds of computer terminals in various geographical locations around the world. A good example of a large network is the Internet, which is a system that allows people from every corner of the globe to access millions of pieces of information about any subject under the sun. Besides varying in size, networks are all at least slightly different in terms of configuration, or what the network is designed to do; businesses customize networks to meet their specific needs. All networks, regardless of size or configuration, experience problems. For example, communications with certain equipment can break down, users might need extra training or forget their passwords, back-up files may be lost, or new software might need to be installed and configured. Whatever the crisis, computer network administrators must know the network system well enough to diagnose and fix the problem.

Computer network administrators or specialists may hold one or several networking responsibilities. The specific job duties assigned to one person depend on the nature and scope of the employer. For example, in a medium-size company that uses computers only minimally, a computer network specialist might be expected to do everything associated with the office computer system. In larger companies with more sophisticated computing systems, computer network administrators are likely to hold narrower and better-defined responsibilities. The following descriptions highlight the different kinds of computer network administrators.

In the narrowest sense, computer network administrators are responsible for adding and deleting files to the *network server,* a centralized computer. Among other things, the server stores the software applications used by network users on a daily basis. Administrators update files from the database, electronic mail, and word-processing applications. They are also responsible for making sure that printing jobs run properly. This task entails telling the server where the printer is and establishing a printing queue, or line, designating which print jobs have priority.

Another duty of some network administrators is setting up user access. Since businesses store confidential information on the server, users typically have access to only a limited number of applications. Network administrators tell the computer who can use which programs and when they can use them. They create a series of passwords to secure the system against internal and external spying. They also troubleshoot problems and questions encountered by staff members.

In companies with large computer systems, *network security specialists* concentrate solely on system security. They set up and monitor user access and update security files as needed. For example, it is very important in universities that only certain administrative personnel have the ability to change student grades on the database. Network security specialists must protect the system from unauthorized grade changes. Network security specialists grant new passwords to users who forget them, record all unauthorized entries, report unauthorized users to appropriate management, and change any files that have been tampered with. They also maintain security files with information about each employee.

Network control operators are in charge of all network communications, most of which operate over telephone lines or fiber optic cables. When users encounter communications problems, they call the network control operator. A typical communications problem is when a user cannot send files to or receive files from other computers. Since users seldom have a high level of technical expertise on the network, the network control operator knows how to ask appropriate questions in user-friendly language to determine the source of the problem. If it is not a user error, the network control operator checks the accuracy of computer files, verifies that modems are functioning properly, and runs noise tests on the communications lines using special equipment. As with all other network specialists, if the problem proves to be too difficult for the network control operator to resolve, he or she seeks help directly from the manufacturer or warranty company.

Network control operators also keep detailed records of the number of communications transactions made, the number and nature of network errors, and the methods used to resolve them. These records help them address problems as they arise in the future.

Network systems administrators who specialize in Internet technology are essential to its success. One of their responsibilities is to prepare servers for use and link them together so others can place things on them. Under the supervision of the *Webmaster,* the systems administrator might set aside areas on a server for particular types of information, such as documents, graphics, or audio. At sites that are set up to handle secure credit card transactions, administrators are responsible for setting up the secure server that handles this job. They also monitor site traffic and take the necessary steps to ensure uninterrupted operation. In some cases, the solution is to provide additional space on the server. In others, the only solution might be to increase bandwidth by upgrading the telephone line linking the site to the Internet.

Requirements

High School

In high school, take as many courses as possible in computer science, mathematics, and science, which provide a solid foundation in computer basics and analytical-thinking skills. You should also practice your verbal and written communication skills in English and speech classes. Business courses are valuable in that they can give you an understanding of how important business decisions, especially those concerning investments in computer equipment, are made.

Postsecondary Training

Most network jobs require at least a bachelor's degree in computer science or computer engineering. More specialized positions require an advanced degree. People with a college education are more likely to deal with the theoretical aspects of computer networking and to be promoted to management positions. Opportunities in computer design, systems analysis, and computer programming, for example, are only open to college graduates. Individuals interested in this field should also pursue postsecondary training in network administration or network engineering.

"I believe that you cannot have enough education and that it should be an ongoing thing," says Nancy Nelson, a network administrator at Baxter Healthcare Corporation in Deerfield, Illinois. "You can learn a lot on your own, but I think you miss out on a lot if you don't get the formal education. Most companies don't even look at a resume that doesn't have a degree. Keeping up with technology can be very rewarding."

Certification or Licensing

Besides the technical/vocational schools that offer courses related to computer networking, several major companies offer professionally taught courses and nationally recognized certification, chief among them are Novell and Microsoft. The Certified Network Professional program supports and complements the aforementioned vendor product certifications. Offered by The Network Professional Association, the program covers fundamental knowledge in client operating systems, microcomputer hardware platforms, network operating system fundamentals, protocols, and topologies. It requires that its students be certified in two specialty areas and have certifications in both.

Commercial postsecondary training programs are flexible. Individuals can complete their courses at their own pace, but must take all parts of the certification test within one year. Students can attend classes at any one of many educational sites around the country or can study on their own. Many students find certification exams difficult.

Other Requirements

Continuing education for any computer profession is crucial to success. Many companies require their computer network administrators to keep up to date on new technological advances by attending classes, workshops, and seminars throughout the year. Also, many companies and professional associations update network specialists through newsletters, other periodicals, and online bulletin boards.

Computer work is complex, detailed, and often very frustrating. Computer network administrators must be well organized and patient. They should enjoy challenges and problem solving and should think logically. They must also be able to communicate complex ideas in simple terms. They have to be able to work well under pressure and deadlines. Like any other computer professionals, network specialists should be naturally curious about the computing field; they must always be willing to learn more about new and different technologies.

Exploring

"One of the greatest learning experiences in this field is just unpacking a new computer, setting it up, and getting connected to the Internet, continually asking yourself how and why as you go," says Dan Creedon, a network administrator at Nesbitt Burns Securities in Chicago.

If you are interested in computer networking, you should join computer clubs at school and community centers and surf the Internet or other online services. Ask your school administration about the possibility of working with the school system's network specialists for a day or longer. Your parents' or friends' employers might also be good places to find this type of opportunity.

If you are seeking part-time jobs, apply for those that include computer work. Though you will not find networking positions, any experience on computers will increase your general computing knowledge. In addition, once employed, you can actively seek exposure to the other computer functions in the business.

You might also try volunteering at local charities that use computer networks in their offices. Since many charities have small budgets, they may offer more opportunities to gain experience with some of the simpler networking tasks. In addition, experiment by creating networks with your own computer, those of your friends, and any printers, modems, and faxes to which you have access.

Basically, you should play around on computers as much as possible. Read and learn from any resource you can, such as magazines, newsletters, and online bulletin boards.

Employers

Any company or organization that uses computer networks in its business employs network administrators. These include insurance companies, banks, financial institutions, healthcare organizations, federal and state governments, universities, and other corporations that rely on networking. Also, since smaller companies are moving to client-server models, more opportunities are becoming available at almost every kind of business.

Starting Out

There are several ways to obtain a position as a computer network specialist. If you are a student in a technical school or university, take advantage of the campus placement office. Check regularly for internship postings, job listings, and notices of on-campus recruitment. Placement offices are also valuable resources for resume tips and interviewing techniques. Internships and summer jobs with corporations are always beneficial and provide experience that will give you the edge over your competition. General computer job fairs are also held throughout the year in larger cities.

The World Wide Web features many online career sites that post job openings, salary surveys, and current employment trends. The Web also has online publications that deal specifically with computer jobs. Interested students can obtain information from computer organizations, such as the IEEE Computer Society and the Network Professional Association.

When a job opportunity arises, you should promptly send a cover letter and resume to the company. Follow up your mailing with a phone call about one week later. If interested, the company recruiter will call to ask questions and possibly arrange an interview. The commercial sponsors of network certification, like Novell and Microsoft, also publish newsletters that list current job openings in the field. The same information is distributed through online bulletin boards and on the Internet as well. In addition, you can scan the classified ads in local newspapers and computer magazines or work with an employment agency to find a position.

Individuals already employed but wishing to move into computer networking should investigate the possibility of tuition reimbursement from their employer for network certification. Many large companies have this type of program, which allows employees to train in a field that would benefit company operations. After successfully completing classes or certification, individuals are better qualified for related job openings in their own companies and are more likely to be hired into them.

Advancement

Advancement options for any computer professional are widely varied. Within the field of networking, administrators and specialists might be promoted to *network managers,* or they can get into network engineering. *Network engineers* design, test, and evaluate network systems, such as LAN, WAN, Internet, and other data communications systems. They also perform modeling, analysis, and planning. Network engineers might also research related products and make hardware and software recommendations.

Network specialists also have the option of going into a different area of computing. They can become *computer programmers, systems analysts, software engineers,* or multimedia professionals. All of these promotions require additional education and solid computer experience.

Earnings

Entry-level computer network administrators earn about $46,000 per year to start. Mid-range salaries, for those with several years of experience and further training, are generally in the mid-fifties. High-range salaries in this field top off around $72,000. These salaries are reserved for individuals with solid experience, additional training, and demonstrated willingness to learn.

Most computer network administrators are employed by companies that offer the full range of benefits, including health insurance, paid vacation, and sick leave. In addition, many companies have tuition reimbursement programs for employees who pursue further education or professional certification.

Work Environment

Computer network administrators work indoors in a comfortable office environment. Their work is generally fast paced and can be frustrating. Some tasks, however, are routine and might get a little boring after awhile. But many times, network specialists are required to work under a lot of pressure. If the network goes down, for example, the company is losing money, and it is the network specialist's job to get the system up and running as fast as possible. The specialist must be able to remember complicated relationships and many details accurately and quickly. Specialists are also called on to deal effectively with the many complaints from network users.

When working on the installation of a new system, many network specialists are required to work overtime until it is fully operational. This usually includes long and frequent meetings. During initial operations of the system, some network specialists may be on-call during other shifts for when problems arise, or they may have to train network users during off hours.

One other potential source of frustration is communication with other employees. Network specialists deal every day with people who usually do not understand the system as well as they do. Network administrators must be able to communicate at different levels of understanding.

Outlook

"Network, or LAN management, is also a hot category, and it's a career that will last beyond the year 2000," according to *Scoring the Best Tech Jobs,* by Susan Gregory Thomas on *U.S. News Online.*

The employment outlook for computer network administrators is expected to be faster than average through 2006, according to the U.S. Department of Labor. Network administrators are in high demand, particularly those with Internet experience.

"Technology is constantly changing," Nancy Nelson says. "It is hard to tell where it will lead in the future. I think that the Internet and all of its pieces will be the place to focus on."

As more and more companies discover the economic and convenience advantages linked to using computer networks at all levels of operation, the demand for well-trained network specialists will increase. Networking positions are likely to grow faster than average as those companies move from mainframe environments to client-server networks.

"I would say that as much as a person is willing to learn is really the amount of advancement opportunities that are open to them," notes Dan Creedon.

For More Information

Association for Computing Machinery
1515 Broadway
New York, NY 10036-5701
Tel: 212-869-7440
Email: SIGS@acm.org
Web: http://www.acm.org

Network Professional Association
710 East Ogden Avenue, Suite 600
Naperville, IL 60563
Tel: 630-579-3282
Email: npa@b-online.com
Web: http://www.npa.org

Computer Programmers

	School Subjects
Computer science Mathematics	

	Personal Skills
Communication/ideas Technical/scientific	

	Work Environment
Primarily indoors Primarily one location	

	Minimum Education Level
Associate's degree	

	Salary Range
$19,520 to $40,100 to $65,200+	

	Certification or Licensing
Voluntary	

	Outlook
Faster than the average	

Overview

Computer programmers work in the field of electronic data processing. They write instructions that tell computers what to do in a computer language, or code, that the computer understands. *Systems programmers* specialize in maintaining the general instructions that control an entire computer system. Maintenance tasks include giving computers instructions on how to allocate time to various jobs they receive from computer terminals and making sure that these assignments are performed properly. There are approximately 568,000 computer programmers employed in the United States.

History

Data processing systems and their support personnel are a product of World War II. The amount of information that had to be compiled and organized for war efforts became so enormous that it was not possible for people to collect it and put it in order in time for the necessary decisions to be made. It was obvious that a quicker way had to be devised to gather and organize information if decisions based on logic and not on guesses were to be made.

After the war, the new computer technology was put to use in other government operations as well as in businesses. The first computer used in a civilian capacity was installed by the Bureau of the Census in 1951 in order to help compile data from the 1950 census. At that time, computers were so large, cumbersome, and energy draining that the only practical use for them was thought to be large projects like the census. However, three years later the first computer was installed by a business firm. Since 1954, many thousands of data processing systems have been installed in government agencies, industrial firms, banks, insurance agencies, educational systems, publishing houses, colleges and universities, and scientific laboratories.

Although computers seem capable of doing just about anything, one thing is still as true of computers today as it was of the first computer 60 years ago—they cannot think for themselves! Computers are machines that can only do exactly what they are told. This requires a small army of qualified computer programmers who understand computer languages well enough to give computers instructions on what to do, when, and how in order to meet the needs of government, business, and individuals. Some programmers are currently working on artificial intelligence, or computers that can in fact "think" for themselves and make humanlike decisions, but perfection of such technology is far off. As long as there are computers and new computer applications, there will be a constant need for programmers.

The Job

Broadly speaking, there are two types of computer programmers: systems programmers and *applications programmers*. Systems programmers maintain the instructions, called programs or software, that control the entire computer system, including both the central processing unit and the equipment with which it communicates, such as terminals, printers, and disk drives. Applications programmers write the software to handle specific jobs and may specialize as engineering and scientific programmers or as business programmers. Some of the latter specialists may be designated *chief business programmers*, who supervise the work of other business programmers.

Programmers are often given program specifications, prepared by systems analysts, that list in detail the steps the computer must follow in order to complete a given task. Programmers then code these instructions in a computer language the computer understands. In smaller companies, analysis and programming may be handled by the same person, called a *programmer-analyst.*

Before actually writing the computer program, a programmer must analyze the work request, understand the current problem and desired resolution, decide on an approach to the problem, and plan what the machine will have to do to produce the required results. Programmers prepare a flowchart to show the steps that the machine must make in sequence. They must pay attention to minute detail and instruct the machine in each step of the process.

These instructions are then coded in one of several programming languages, such as BASIC, COBOL, FORTRAN, PASCAL, RPG, CSP, or C++. When the program is completed, the programmer tests its working practicality by running it on simulated data. If the machine responds according to expectations, actual data will be fed into it and the program will be activated. If the computer does not respond as anticipated, the program will have to be debugged—that is, examined for errors that must be eliminated. Finally, the programmer prepares an instruction sheet for the computer operator who will run the program.

The programmer's job concerns both an overall picture of the problem at hand and the minute detail of potential solutions. Programmers work from two points of view: from that of the people who need certain results and from that of technological problem solving. The work is divided equally between meeting the needs of other people and comprehending the capabilities of the machines.

Electronic data systems involve more than just one machine. Depending upon the kind of system being used, the operation may require other machines such as printers or other peripherals. Introducing a new piece of equipment to an existing system often requires programmers to rewrite many programs.

Programmers may specialize in certain types of work, depending on the kind of problem to be solved and on the employer. For example, making a program for a payroll is very different from programming the study of structures of chemical compounds. Programmers who specialize in a certain field or industry generally have education or experience in that area before they are promoted to senior programming positions. *Information system programmers* specialize in programs for storing and retrieving physical science, engineering, or medical information; text analysis; and language, law, military, or library science data. As the information superhighway continues to grow, information system programmers will have increased opportunities in online businesses, such as those of Lexis/Nexis, Westlaw, America Online, Microsoft, and many others.

Process control programmers develop programs for systems that control automatic operations for commercial and industrial enterprises, such as steelmaking, sanitation plants, combustion systems, computerized production testing, or automatic truck loading. *Numerical control tool programmers* program the tape that controls the machining of automatic machine tools.

Requirements

High School

In high school you should take any computer programming or computer science courses available. You should also concentrate on math, science, and schematic drawing courses, since these subjects directly prepare students for careers in computer programming.

Postsecondary Training

Most employers prefer their programmers to be college graduates. In the past, as the field was first taking shape, employers were known to hire people with some formal education and little or no experience but with determination and aptitude to learn quickly. As the market becomes saturated with individuals wishing to break into this field, however, a college degree is becoming increasingly important.

Many personnel officers administer aptitude tests to determine potential for programming work. Some employers send new employees to computer schools or in-house training sessions before they are considered qualified to assume programming responsibilities. Training periods may last as long as a few weeks, months, or even a year.

Many junior and community colleges also offer two-year associate's degree programs in data processing, computer programming, and other computer-related technologies.

Most four-year colleges and universities have computer science departments with a variety of computer-related majors, any of which could prepare a student for a career in programming. Employers who require a college degree often do not express a preference as to major field of study, although mathematics or computer science is highly favored. Other acceptable majors may be business administration, accounting, engineering, or physics. Entrance requirements for jobs with the government are much the same as those in private industry.

Certification or Licensing

Students who choose to obtain a two-year degree might consider becoming certified by the Institute for Certification of Computing Professionals, whose address is listed at the end of this article. Although it is not required, certification may boost an individual's attractiveness to employers during the job search.

Other Requirements

Personal qualifications such as a high degree of reasoning ability, patience, and persistence, as well as aptitude for mathematics, are important for computer programmers. Some employers whose work is highly technical require that programmers be qualified in the area in which the firm or agency operates. Engineering firms, for example, prefer young people with an engineering background and are willing to train them in some programming techniques. For other firms, such as banks, consumer-level knowledge of the services that they offer may be sufficient background for incoming programmers.

Exploring

If you are interested in becoming a computer programmer, you might visit a large bank or insurance company in the community and seek an appointment to talk with one of the programmers on the staff. You may be able to visit the data processing center and see the machines in operation. You might also talk with a sales representative from one of the large manufacturers of data processing equipment and request whatever brochures or pamphlets the company publishes.

It is a good idea to start early and get some hands-on experience operating and programming a computer. A trip to the local library or bookstore is likely to turn up countless books on programming; this is one field where the resources to teach yourself are highly accessible and available for all levels of competency. Joining a computer club and reading professional magazines are other ways to become more familiar with this career field. In addition, you should start exploring the Internet, itself a great source of information about computer-related careers.

High school and college students who can operate a computer may be able to obtain part-time jobs in business computer centers or in some larger companies. Any computer experience will be helpful for future computer training.

Employers

Computer programmers work for manufacturing companies, data processing service firms, hardware and software companies, banks, insurance companies, credit companies, publishing houses, government agencies, and colleges and universities throughout the country. Many programmers are employed by businesses as consultants on a temporary or contractual basis.

Starting Out

You can look for an entry-level programming position in the same way as most other jobs; there is no special or standard point of entry into the field. Individuals with the necessary qualifications should apply directly to companies, agencies, or industries that have announced job openings through a school placement office, an employment agency, or the classified ads.

Students in two- or four-year degree programs should work closely with their schools' placement offices, since major local employers often list job openings exclusively with such offices.

If the market for programmers is particularly tight, you may want to obtain an entry-level job with a large corporation or computer software firm, even if the job does not include programming. As jobs in the programming department open up, current employees in other departments are often the first to know, and are favored over nonemployees during the interviewing process. Getting a foot in the door in this way has proven to be successful for many programmers.

Advancement

Programmers are ranked—according to education, experience, and level of responsibility—as junior or senior programmers. After programmers have attained the highest available programming position, they can choose to make one of several career moves in order to be promoted still higher.

Some programmers are more interested in the analysis aspect of computing than the actual charting and coding of programming. They often acquire additional training and experience in order to prepare themselves for promotion to positions as systems programmers or systems analysts. These individuals have the added responsibility of working with upper management to define equipment and cost guidelines for a specific project. They perform only broad programming tasks, leaving most of the detail work to programmers.

Other programmers become more interested in administration and management and may wish to become heads of programming departments. They tend to be more people-oriented and enjoy leading others to excellence. As the level of management responsibilities increases, the amount of technical work performed decreases, so management positions are not for everyone.

Still other programmers may branch out into different technical areas, such as total computer operations, hardware design, and software or network engineering. With experience, they may be placed in charge of the data systems center. They may also decide to go to work for a consulting company, work that generally pays extremely well.

Programming provides a solid background in the computer industry. Experienced programmers enjoy a wide variety of possibilities for career advancement. The hardest part for programmers usually is deciding exactly what they want to do.

Earnings

According to the National Association of Colleges and Employers, the average 1997 starting salary for college graduates employed in the private sector was about $35,167. Salaries for experienced programmers averaged $40,100 a year; some earned more than $65,200. Programmers employed by the federal government were paid between $19,520 and $24,180, depending on their academic record. Programmers in the West and the North are generally paid more than those in the South. This is because most big computer companies are located in the Silicon Valley in northern California or in the state of Washington, where Microsoft, a major employer of programmers, has its headquarters. Also, some industries, like public utilities and data processing service firms, tend to pay their programmers higher wages than do other types of employers, such as banks and schools.

Most programmers receive the customary paid vacation and sick leave and are included in such company benefits as group insurance and retirement benefit plans.

Work Environment

Most programmers work in pleasant office conditions since computers require an air-conditioned, dust-free environment. Programmers perform most of their duties in one primary location but may be asked to travel to other computing sites on occasion.

The average programmer works between 35 and 40 hours weekly. In some job situations, the programmer may have to work nights or weekends on short notice. This might happen when a program is going through its trial runs, for example, or when there are many demands for additional services.

Outlook

Employment opportunities for computer programmers should increase faster than the average through 2006, according to the U.S. Department of Labor. Employment growth will be strong because businesses, scientific organizations, government agencies, and schools continue to look for new applications for computers and to make improvements in software already in use. Also, there is a need to develop complex operating programs that can use higher-level computer languages and can network with other computer equipment and systems.

Job applicants with the best chances of employment will be college graduates with a knowledge of several programming languages, especially newer ones used for computer networking and database management. In addition, the best applicants will have some training or experience in an applied field such as accounting, science, engineering, or management. Competition for jobs will be heavier among graduates of two-year data processing programs and among people with equivalent experience or with less training. Since this field is constantly changing, programmers should stay abreast of the latest technology to remain competitive.

──────────────For More Information

For more information about careers in computer programming, contact:

Association for Computing Machinery
One Astor Plaza
1515 Broadway
New York, NY 10036
Tel: 212-869-7440
Email: ACMHELP@acm.org
Web: http://www.acm.org

Association of Information Technology Professionals
315 South Northwest Highway, Suite 200
Park Ridge, IL 60068-4278
Tel: 800-224-9371
Email: 70430.35@compuserve.com
Web: http://www.aitp.org

For information on certification programs, contact:

Institute for Certification of Computing Professionals
2200 East Devon Avenue, Suite 247
Des Plaines, IL 60018
Tel: 800-843-8422
Email: 74040.3722@compuserve.com
Web: http://www.iccp.org

Computer Systems/Programmer Analysts

Overview

Computer systems/programmer analysts first analyze the computing needs of a business and then design a new system or upgrade an old system to meet those needs. The position can be split between two people, the *systems programmer* and the *systems analyst,* but is frequently held by just one person who oversees the work from beginning to end.

History

The first major advances in modern computer technology were made during World War II. After the war, people thought that computers were too big (they easily filled entire warehouses) to ever be used for anything other than government projects, such as the processing of the 1950 Census.

The introduction of semiconductors to computer technology made possible smaller and less expensive computers. The semiconductors replaced the bigger, slower vacuum tubes of the first computers. These changes made it easier for businesses to adapt computers to their needs, which they began doing as early as 1954. Within 30 years, computers had revolutionized the way people work, play, and even shop. Today, computers are everywhere, from businesses of all kinds, to government agencies, charitable organizations, and private homes. Over the years, technology has continued to shrink computer size and increase speed at an unprecedented rate.

The need for systems/programmer analysts grew out of the proliferation of hardware and software products on the market. While many offices have an unofficial "computer expert," whose main job may be in accounting or word processing or office administration, most medium-size to larger companies that have invested in expensive computer systems have found the need to employ, either full time or on a consulting basis, a systems analyst or programmer analyst.

In addition, the computer revolution brought with it awareness that choosing the appropriate system from the start is crucial to business success. Purchasing decisions are based on many complicated scientific and mathematical models as well as on practical business sense. Therefore, systems analysts have become essential to business decision making.

Businesses and organizations also discovered that, like all other new technologies, computer systems break down a lot. It has become more cost effective for many organizations to have full-time systems analysts on site than to call computer repairers to fix every little glitch.

The Job

Businesses invest hundreds of thousands of dollars in computer systems to make their operations more efficient and thus more profitable. As older systems become obsolete, businesses are also faced with the task of replacing them or upgrading them with new technology. Computer systems/programmer analysts plan and develop new computer systems or upgrade existing systems to meet changing business needs. They also install, modify, and maintain functioning computer systems. The process of choosing and implementing a computer system is similar for programmer analysts who work for very different employers. However, specific decisions in terms of hardware and software differ depending on the industry.

The first stage of the process involves meeting with management and users in order to discuss the problem at hand. For example, a company's accounting system might be slow, unreliable, and generally outdated. During many hours of meetings, systems/programmer analysts and management discuss various options, including commercial software, hardware upgrades, and customizing possibilities that may solve the problems. At the end of the discussions, which may last as long as several weeks or months, the programmer analyst defines the specific system goals as agreed upon by the participants.

Next, systems/programmer analysts engage in highly analytic and logical activities. They use tools like structural analysis, data modeling, mathematics, and cost accounting to determine which computers, including hardware and software and peripherals, will be required to meet the goals of the project. They must consider the trade-offs between extra efficiency and speed and increased costs. Weighing the pros and cons of each additional system feature is an important factor in system planning. Whatever preliminary decisions are made, they must be supported by mathematical and financial evidence.

As the final stage of the planning process, systems/programmer analysts prepare reports and formal presentations to be delivered to management. Reports must be written in clear, concise language that business professionals, who are not necessarily technical experts, can understand thoroughly. Formal presentations in front of groups of various sizes are often required as part of the system proposal.

If the system or the system upgrades are approved, equipment is purchased and installed. Then, the programmer analysts get down to the real technical work so that all the different computers and peripherals function well together. They prepare specifications, diagrams, and other programming structures, and perhaps using CASE (computer-aided systems engineering) technology, they write the new or upgraded programming code. If they work solely as systems analysts, it is at this point that they hand over all of their information to the systems programmer so that he or she can begin to write the programming code.

Systems design and programming involves defining the files and records to be accessed by the system, outlining the processing steps, and suggesting formats for output that meet the needs of the company. User-friendliness of the front-end applications is extremely important for user productivity. Therefore, programmer analysts must be able to envision how nontechnical system users view their on-screen work. Systems/programmer analysts might also specify security programs that allow only authorized personnel access to certain files or groups of files.

As the programming is written, programmer analysts set up test runs of various parts of the system, making sure each step of the way that major goals are reached. Once the system is up and running, problems, or bugs, begin to pop up. Programmer analysts are responsible for debugging. They must isolate the problem and review the hundreds of lines of programming commands to determine where the mistake is located. Then they must enter the correct command or code and recheck the program.

Depending on the employer, some systems/programmer analysts might be involved with computer networking. Network communication programs tell two or more computers or peripherals how to work with each other. When a system is composed of equipment from various manufacturers, networking is essential for smooth system functioning. For example, shared printers have to know how to order print jobs as they come in from various terminals. Some programmer analysts write the code that establishes printing queues. Others might be involved in user training since they know the software applications well. They might also customize commercial software programs to meet the needs of their company.

Many programmer analysts become specialized in an area of business, science, or engineering. They seek education and further on-the-job training in these areas to develop expertise. They may therefore attend special seminars, workshops, and classes designed for their needs. This extra knowledge allows them to develop a deeper understanding of the computing problems specific to the business or industry.

Requirements

High School

A bachelor's degree in computer science is a minimum requirement for systems/programmer analysts. If you are interested in this career, in high school you should take as many math, science, and computer classes as possible. These courses provide a foundation of basic concepts and encourage the development of analytical and logical thinking skills. Since programmer analysts do a lot of proposal writing that may or may not be technical in nature,

English classes are valuable as well. Speech classes will help prepare you for making formal presentations to management and clients.

Postsecondary Training

Course work in preparation for this field includes math, computer programming, science, and logic. Several years of related work experience, including knowledge of programming languages, are often necessary as well. For some very high-level positions, an advanced degree in a specific computer subfield may be required. Also, depending on the employer, proficiency in business, science, or engineering may be necessary.

Certification or Licensing

Some programmer analysts pursue certification through the Institute for Certification of Computing Professionals. In particular, they take classes and exams to become certified systems professionals (CSPs). Certification is voluntary and is an added credential for job hunters. CSPs have achieved a recognized level of knowledge and experience in principles and practices related to systems.

Other Requirements

Successful systems/programmer analysts demonstrate strong analytical skills and enjoy the challenges of problem solving. They are able to understand problems that exist on many levels, from a very technical problem to a more practical, business-oriented one. They can visualize complicated and abstract relationships between computer hardware and software and are good at matching needs to equipment.

Programmer analysts have to be flexible as well. They routinely deal with many different kinds of people, from management to data entry clerks. Therefore, they must be knowledgeable in a lot of functional areas of the company. They should be able to talk to management about cost-effective solutions, to programmers about detailed coding, and to clerks about user-friendliness of the applications.

As is true for all computer professionals, systems/programmer analysts must be able to learn about new technologies quickly. They should be naturally curious about keeping up on cutting-edge developments; keeping up can be time-consuming. Furthermore, they are often so busy at their jobs that staying in the know is done largely on their own time.

Exploring

If you are interested, you have several options to learn more about what it is like to be a computer systems/programmer analyst. You can spend a day with a working professional in this field in order to experience firsthand a typical day. Career days of this type can usually be arranged through school guidance counselors or the public relations managers of local corporations.

Strategy games, including chess, played with friends or school clubs are good ways to put your analytical thinking skills to use while having fun. Commercial games range in themes from war simulations to world historical development. When choosing a game, the key is to make sure it relies on qualities similar to those used by programmer analysts.

Last, you should become a computer hobbyist and learn everything you can about computers by working and playing with them on a daily basis. Surfing the Internet regularly, as well as reading trade magazines, will also be helpful. You might also want to try hooking up a mini system at home or school, configuring terminals, printers, modems, and other peripherals into a coherent system. This activity requires a fair amount of knowledge and so should be supervised by a professional.

Employers

Computer systems/programmer analysts work for all types of firms and organizations that do their work on computers. Such companies may include manufacturing companies, data processing service firms, hardware and software companies, banks, insurance companies, credit companies, publishing houses, government agencies, and colleges and universities. Many programmer analysts are employed by businesses as consultants on a temporary or contractual basis.

Starting Out

Since systems/programmer analysts typically have at least some experience in a computer-related job, most are hired into these positions from lower-level ones within the same company. For example, programmers, software engineering technicians, and network and database administrators all gain valuable computing experience that can be put to good use at a systems job. Alternatively, individuals who acquire expertise in systems programming and analysis while in other jobs may want to work with a headhunter to find the right systems positions for them. Also, trade magazines, newspapers, and employment agencies regularly feature job openings in this field. Another source of job information is Career Mosaic on the World Wide Web. Career Mosaic is a service that makes access to various companies' job listings easier and faster.

Students in four-year degree programs should work closely with their schools' placement offices. Companies regularly work through such offices in order to find the best-qualified graduates. Since it may be difficult to find a job as a programmer analyst to begin with, it is important for students to consider their long-term potential within a certain company. The chance for promotion into a systems job can make lower-level jobs more appealing, at least in the short run. The educational reimbursement policy of the company is another important consideration, since it can enable individuals to achieve the educational requirements of systems jobs inexpensively.

For those individuals already employed in a computer-related job but wanting to get into systems programming and analysis, additional formal education is a good idea. Some employers without educational policies may be willing to pay for such training if it could directly benefit the business.

Advancement

Systems/programmer analysts already occupy a relatively high-level technical job. Promotion, therefore, usually occurs in one of two directions. First, programmer analysts can be put in charge of increasingly larger and more complex systems. Instead of concentrating on a local system—for example, the corporate services systems—an analyst can oversee all company systems and networks. This kind of technically based promotion can also put systems/programmer analysts into other areas of computing. With the proper experience and additional training, they can get into database or network management and design, software engineering, or even quality assurance.

The other direction in which programmer analysts can go is managerial. Depending on the position sought, formal education—either a bachelor's degree in business or a master's in business administration—may be required. As more administrative duties are added, more technical ones are taken away. Therefore, programmer analysts who enjoy the technical aspect of their work more than anything else may not want to pursue this advancement track. Excellent computing managers have both a solid background in various forms of computing and a good grasp of what it takes to run a department. Also, having the vision to see how technology will change in the short and long terms and how those changes will affect the industry concerned is a quality of a good manager.

Earnings

According to the U.S. Department of Labor, annual salaries for systems/programmer analysts averaged about $46,300 in 1996. Fifty percent earned from $34,000 to $59,000 a year. Salaries are slightly higher in geographic areas where many computer companies are clustered, like northern California and Seattle, Washington. According to the National Association of Colleges and Employers, programmer analysts with a bachelor's degree earned an average of $39,722 a year; those holding a master's degree or higher earned from $44,734 to $63,367 a year.

Most programmer analysts receive health insurance, paid vacation time, and sick leave. Some employers offer tuition reimbursement programs and in-house computer training workshops.

Work Environment

Computer systems/programmer analysts work in comfortable office environments. If they work as consultants, they may travel frequently. Otherwise, travel is limited to trade shows, seminars, and visits to vendors for demonstrations. They might also visit other businesses to observe their systems in action.

Programmer analysts usually work 40-hour weeks and enjoy the regular holiday schedule of days off. However, as deadlines for system installation, upgrades, and debugging approach, they are often required to work overtime in order to meet them. Extra compensation for overtime hours may come in the form of time-and-a-half pay or compensatory time off, depending on the precise nature of the employee's duties, company policy, and state law. If the employer operates off-shifts, programmer analysts may be on-call to address any problems that might arise at any time of the day or night. This is relatively rare in the service sector but more common in manufacturing, heavy industry, and data processing firms.

Computer systems programming and analysis is very detailed work. The tiniest error can cause major system disruptions, which can be a great source of frustration. Systems/programmer analysts must be prepared to deal with this frustration and be able to work well under pressure.

Outlook

The U.S. Department of Labor predicts that the occupation of computer systems/programmer analyst will be one of the three fastest growing careers through 2006. Increases are mainly a product of the growing number of businesses that rely extensively on computers. When businesses automate, their daily operations depend on the capacity of their computer systems to perform at desired levels. The development of new technology and the need for businesses to network their information will add to the demand for qualified programmer analysts. Businesses will rely increasingly on systems/programmer analysts to make the right purchasing decisions and to keep systems running smoothly.

Many computer manufacturers are beginning to expand the range of services they offer to business clients. In the years to come, they may hire many systems/programmer analysts to work as consultants on a per-project basis with a potential client. These workers would perform essentially the same duties, with the addition of extensive follow-up maintenance. They would analyze business needs and suggest proper systems to answer them. In addition, more and more independent consulting firms are hiring systems/programmer analysts to perform the same tasks.

Programmer analysts with advanced degrees in computer science, management information systems, or computer engineering, will be in great demand. MBAs with emphasis in information systems will also be highly desirable.

For More Information

For more information about systems/programmer analyst positions, contact the following organizations:

Association for Systems Management
1433 West Bagley Road
PO Box 38370
Cleveland, OH 44138
Tel: 216-234-2930

Association of Information Technology Professionals
315 South Northwest Highway, Suite 200
Park Ridge, IL 60068-4278
Tel: 800-224-9371
Email: 70430.35@compuserve.com
Web: http://www.aitp.org

For more information on related certification, contact:

Institute for Certification of Computing Professionals
2200 East Devon Avenue, Suite 247
Des Plaines, IL 60018
Tel: 800-843-8422
Email: 74040.3722@compuserve.com
Web: http://www.iccp.org

Computer Trainers

	School Subjects
Computer science Speech	
	Personal Skills
Helping/teaching Technical/scientific	
	Work Environment
Primarily indoors Primarily multiple locations	
	Minimum Education Level
Bachelor's degree	
	Salary Range
$36,500 to $47,400 to $57,800	
	Certification or Licensing
Recommended	
	Outlook
Much faster than the average	

Overview

Computer trainers teach topics related to all aspects of using computers in the workplace, including personal computer (PC) software; operating systems for both stand-alone and networked systems; management tools for networks; enterprise software that enables efficient management of large corporations' production, sales, and information systems; software applications and operating systems for mainframe computers and customized software for specific industry management. Some trainers work for training companies, others for software developers. Another segment of trainers is comprised of consultants. There are also companies that produce training materials, including disk-based multimedia technology-delivered learning, instructor-led courseware, skills assessment, videos, and classroom teaching manuals.

History

The worldwide market for information technology (IT) education and training was estimated at $18.8 billion in 1998, up from $14.7 billion in 1996, according to International Data Corporation. Computer skills training was ranked the number-one training category in 1997 by a national executive survey and was forecasted to continue to place in the top three for years to come, according to the American Society for Training and Development (ASTD).

The field of computer training has been around since about 1983, when the computer industry exploded with the introduction of the first PCs. With all of the new software packages being released, individual IT and information services (IS) departments could not possibly keep up with the amount of training their employees needed. Software vendor companies started sending their employees out to teach new purchasers how to use their products, and a new section of the computer industry was born.

In the beginning, computer training was conducted like any other training, in a classroom setting with an instructor. Although classroom training is still prevalent today, "Now, that landscape is awash with a torrent of new technologies, creating almost limitless possibilities for heightened learning," according to "Training Industry Trends 1997," by Laurie J. Bassi, Scott Cheney, and Mark Van Buren of the ASTD. "These days, a variety of electronic media can facilitate the transfer of knowledge and skills. That represents both a challenge and an opportunity for professionals who specialize in workplace learning and performance. Technological innovation is constantly and pervasively altering the way in which work is done. That, in turn, has immediate consequences for the demands on specialists in workplace learning and performance improvement. The rapid pace of change requires that workplace learning occur on a just-in-time, just-what's-needed, and just-where-it's-needed basis."

Computer trainers are turning to that technology to deliver their instructions. Developments in hardware, computer networking, multimedia software, and video conferencing have tremendous potential for multiple-site instruction and training closer to people's work sites, according to the ASTD. The organization also notes that training departments are finding new ways to deliver services by using support networks of internal and external training providers, including consultants, community colleges, and universities.

The Job

The field of computer training encompasses several different areas. *Software vendor trainers* work for developer companies. Consultants work for themselves as independent contractors, often specializing in certain computer languages, skills, or platforms. Some trainers work in the corporate training departments of companies that develop products other than computers and software. Others are teachers and professors.

"As a software trainer, my duties are to be prepared to teach various topics related to our software to a variety of clients on any given day," says Marcy Anderson, a software trainer for Cyborg Systems, a human-resource software developer. "I teach from a training manual and demonstrate the procedures on my computer that displays the information on a large screen for the entire class. The class is given assignments throughout the day that they complete on their PCs. I assist them one-on-one with their questions as the class continues. Cyborg has a training center with four classrooms. I conduct classes in the training center, or I travel to the client and hold classes on-site."

Consultant trainers are certified to teach several different products, applications, environments, and databases, usually with companies such as Microsoft, IBM, or Apple. Most have been in the computer industry for many years, previously working as software programmers, architects, project managers, or developers.

Whatever their affiliation, most computer trainers use several ways to disseminate learning technologies, including CD-ROM, CBT-Text, electronic performance support systems, the Internet, Intranets, multimedia presentations, and video conferencing.

One of the most important things for trainers to have is certification for the courses they intend to instruct. The International Board of Standards for Training, Performance, and Instruction has an outline of ground-level skills that are mandatory for technical trainers, according to the ASTD. The following 14 competencies are the basis for the certified trainer examination. For trainers to receive certification, they must show proof that they can execute the following:

1. Analyze course materials and learning information.
2. Ensure preparation of the instructional site.
3. Establish and maintain instructor credibility.
4. Manage the learning environment.
5. Demonstrate effective communication skills.
6. Demonstrate effective presentation skills.
7. Demonstrate effective questioning skills and techniques.
8. Respond appropriately to learners' needs for clarification or feedback.
9. Provide positive reinforcement and motivational incentives.

10. Use instructional methods appropriately.
11. Use media effectively.
12. Evaluate learner performance.
13. Evaluate instruction delivery.
14. Report evaluation information.

Trainers are beginning to explore the field of online learning. In the article, "Our Turn-of-the-Century Trend Watch," Paul Clothier, senior instructor, Softwire Corporation, says that "Improved online learning (OL) design and technologies will significantly impact the technical training profession over the next few years. At present, much of the technical training taking place is in the form of instructor-led training (ILT) in a classroom. There are many advantages to ILT, but there are also considerable disadvantages, such as time investment, travel, and expense. To get a group of your most valuable technical people off to a week of training is often a major expense and inconvenience. Organizations are crying out for a better alternative, and OL increasingly is seen as an option."

Requirements

High School

If you are interested in a career in computer training, take as many computer and mathematics classes as possible in high school. These will provide the foundation for the rest of your computer education. Start learning about computer programs, such as Visual Basic, on your own. Speech, drama, or other performance courses will also help get you used to speaking in front of a crowd. "A little showmanship doesn't hurt in keeping the class interested," notes Marcy.

Postsecondary Training

While there is no universally accepted way to prepare for a job in computer training, a bachelor's degree is generally required by most employers, but it is not set in stone which major is the best for this field. Some majors that share skills with training include computer science, business, and education.

To teach some of the more complex systems, a graduate degree might be necessary.

"In my personal experience, I did not pursue an education degree to become a trainer," says Marcy. "I have a business degree and years of experience in the human resources field. For software training, though, knowledge of software and computers is essential. A degree in education would provide excellent skills for this type of position. Additionally, a business or liberal arts major might provide the presentation skills that are valuable. Certainly any presentation or public speaking certifications would be desirable."

Obtaining graduate and postgraduate degrees enhances potential marketability, as well as future salaries.

Certification or Licensing

Trainers should be certified in the products (such as Microsoft C++, MFC, Visual Basic, and Access), developments (including Internet, HTML, Java Script), applications (MS Office, for example), environments (such as OS/2, Windows, client/server), and databases (including ADO, Access, ODBC, BD/2, and SQL) they want to teach. Classes in each of the disciplines are available from the manufacturers, and students must pass an examination before receiving certification. Trainers who are employed by hardware and software developers might receive on-the-job instruction on the most current product releases. Certification is not mandatory (except for consultants), but it will provide job seekers with competitive advantages.

Technological advances come so rapidly in the computer field that continuous study is necessary even for trainers to keep skills up-to-date. Continuing education is usually offered by employers, hardware and software vendors, colleges and universities, or private training institutions. Additional training can also come from professional associations, such as the ASTD.

Other Requirements

"Trainers need to be patient and extroverted," says Marcy. "A sense of humor is essential, along with a high level of energy. People who are very introverted, even though they might be good with computers, should not do software training." Trainers also have to be ready to teach any class in their repertoire at any time, so they have to be adaptable and flexible to handle that uncertainty.

Exploring

One way to begin exploring this field now is to talk to someone who is a computer trainer. Marcy also suggests getting involved in speech or drama clubs. "Any experiences a high schooler can get in making presentations or performing in front of a group help to build the skills necessary to be successful in this career," she says.

Internships are always helpful ways of obtaining some experience in the field before graduation. Having a job in the training department of a large corporation or software vendor would provide invaluable experience and contacts.

Teach yourself the various software packages, and read as much as you can about the industry. Although jobs in the computer industry are abundant, there is always competition for desirable positions.

Employers

Computer trainers are employed by various sources, from large, international companies to community colleges. Many work for hardware and software manufacturers or training departments in the bigger companies. Others are employed by training companies that disseminate training information and tools. Still other computer trainers work independently as consultants. The rest are employed by schools, adult continuing education programs, and government institutions. Some software companies and consultants operate training sites on the Internet. Since almost every type of company will need computer training at one point or another, these companies are located throughout the country, and, indeed, throughout the world.

Starting Out

There are several ways to obtain a position as a computer trainer. Some people are hired right out of college by software companies. "There are many software companies that hire smart college grads to work with clients and implement their software," notes Marcy. Others start out in technical positions with software companies then move into training as their expertise in the product increases.

Job candidates for computer trainer positions might obtain their jobs from on-campus recruitment, classified want ads, posting their resume on the Internet, or word of mouth. Many large cities hold technology job fairs that host hundreds of companies, all of which are interested in hiring.

Advancement

Computer trainers can move upward into positions such as training specialists, senior training specialists, and training managers, depending on the size of the company.

Earnings

The average training specialist earned $40,300 in 1996, according to the 1996 Information Systems Compensation Survey, compiled by William M. Mercer Inc. Senior training specialists averaged $47,400 per year, and training managers earned $57,000. In general, salaries in the area of computer trainers increased with the level of education. The average salary for managers with postgraduate degrees was significantly larger than average, totaling $52,111, according to the 1996 Service News Salary Survey.

The most certain way for training specialists to improve their value is to complete a certification program, states Service News. "The average salaries for specialists carrying certifications from Compaq, Lotus, Hewlett-Packard, Apple, IBM, A+/CompTIA, and Novell were all well above the average for this group. Specialists who hold no certification earned an average of $36,500, which is about $3,000 below the overall average earnings for the specialists responding to the survey."

Service News notes that for training managers, the size of the company played a large role in the average wages. Those working in firms with more than 100,000 employees reported average earnings of $57,800, whereas those in companies with 50 to 200 employees reported an average wage of $40,168.

Most computer trainers who are employed by corporations receive medical and dental insurance, paid vacations, sick days, and yearly bonuses. Bonuses for training specialists averaged $1,600. Senior training specialists received $2,500, and training managers were awarded $5,200 on average in 1996.

Work Environment

Computer trainers normally work in offices in comfortable surroundings. They usually work 40 hours a week, which is the same as many other professional or office workers. However, travel to clients' sites can be required and might increase the number of hours worked per week. They spend most of their time in classrooms or training facilities. "The best part of the job is that it is interesting and fun," says Marcy. "It is nice to be an 'expert' and impart knowledge to others, even though it can be hard sometimes to feel up and energized to teach every day."

Outlook

The field of computers is expected to grow much faster than average through the year 2006. Consequently, there will be a great need for computer trainers as the technology continues to develop. Information from the EQW National Employer Survey indicates that employers are using a variety of external training providers. As this outsourcing grows, an increase in the number of training providers is likely. Such independent providers as community and technical colleges, universities, profit-oriented learning and development centers, and private industry associations will all be discovering new business opportunities in outsourcing, according to the ASTD. "The short life cycles of technology products, compounded by the greater complexity of many job roles, are expected to heighten the demand for external information-technology education providers and other training providers," the ASTD notes.

For More Information

For a list of academic programs and resources in the training field, contact the following:

American Society for Training and Development
1640 King Street, Box 1443
Alexandria, VA 22313-2043
Tel: 703-683-8100
Web: http://www.astd.org

International Association of Information Technology Trainers
9810 Patuxent Woods Drive
Columbia, MD 21046-1561
Tel: 410-290-7000
Web: http://www.itrain.org

International Board of Standards for Training, Performance and Instruction Web Site
Web: http://www.ibstpi.org

Multimedia and Internet Training Newsletter/brandon-hall.com
Web: http://www.multimediatraining.com/index.shtml

Data Processing Technicians

School Subjects	Business Computer science Mathematics
Personal Skills	Communication/ideas Technical/scientific
Work Environment	Primarily indoors Primarily one location
Minimum Education Level	Associate's degree
Salary Range	$18,000 to $30,000 to $33,000
Certification or Licensing	Voluntary
Outlook	About as fast as the average

Overview

Data processing technicians use computers to manage and store information. They provide complex and detailed information necessary to daily office operations in business and government. With computers they can organize and analyze data, perform mathematical calculations, and provide data for some scientific or engineering design problems. Data processing technicians work with many different kinds of professionals including information scientists; systems analysts; information processing engineers; and engineering, scientific, and business *computer programmers*.

History

The field of electronic data processing is relatively new. Forerunners of today's modern computers were not developed until the 1930s, and the first all-electronic general-purpose computer was not completed until 1946. This computer was called ENIAC (Electronic Numerical Integrator and Calculator) and was huge in size, using eighteen thousand vacuum tubes. In 1951, the U.S. census was processed by computer for the first time; in 1954, the computer moved into private businesses. Since then, public and private industries, universities, and other research centers have developed many new and different kinds of computers. These technological advances have enabled people to solve problems faster and more accurately than ever before.

Recent developments in electronics have made it possible to build miniature digital computers, minicomputers, and microprocessors at progressively lower costs. Consequently, there has been a dramatic increase in the number of companies that use computers regularly for factory and office automation, scientific and medical research, robotics, aerospace engineering, and word and information processing. No other single technological innovation (except for television) has had a greater impact on the changing American scene than the computer.

The Job

Although many tasks overlap with what is considered programming on the high end and data entry on the low end, there are basically two types of data processing occupations. Data processing technicians who work primarily with the daily activities of business, such as payroll and accounting, are one type. This work requires knowledge of business administration as well as specialized training in computer operations, programming concepts, and modern management accounting techniques. The second type is scientific data processing. It requires knowledge of mathematics, physical science, or engineering as well as specialized courses in analysis techniques, computer programming concepts, and statistical analysis.

A data processing technician in a medium-size or large company might be responsible for producing a sales report each week. The accountants and data entry clerks have already entered the details of individual sales into the computer system, but managers are usually not interested in this level of detail. Instead, they prefer to read a report that summarizes and analyzes sales activity for a certain time period. A data processing technician gives the computer instructions on how to convert the sales information into the necessary format and perform related calculations on it. The technician knows enough about computer programming to run these kinds of reports, but not necessarily enough to create large-scale computer programs from scratch.

The personnel in large data processing centers generally include *machine operators* and data processing technicians, who may in some cases also be called *junior programmers* or *programmers* depending on their level of responsibility. Machine operators are usually not officially considered technicians, although some companies might give operators duties related to data processing. These positions are normally suitable as entry-level positions for individuals wishing to become technicians, however. Data processing technicians generally have more education and experience than do machine operators.

Business problems arise every day, and computer programs are designed to deal with them. *Senior programmers* and *analysts* first define the problem in detail and identify the relationships among all factors to be considered. They must know about different types of computers, computer languages, and data processing procedures.

Data processing technicians receive an analysis of the problem, the computer system and units to be used, and the required computer language as an assignment from the analyst and the senior programmer. The technicians then design the necessary flowcharts and input-output forms. They collect necessary data and fill in some details of the program, or set of instructions, to enter into the computer.

In addition to providing details for new programs, data processing technicians modify existing programs to meet new requirements or increase operating efficiency. A technician may share an office with as many as three or four other technicians or programmers. Technicians also spend considerable time in the computer room, checking on programs to be certain they have no errors and that the answers coming from the program are correct. They might also supervise machine operators or data entry clerks.

After the program runs for the first time, the programmers and technicians analyze the results. Quite often, a small error in programming can cause a big problem in results. It is the technician's responsibility to discover and correct mistakes, a process called *debugging*. When the debugging has been completed, the program is ready to run regularly, and the technicians can turn their attention to other problems.

Scientific or *business data processing technicians* spend most of their time studying data and methods of defining problems and solutions to problems that are specific to their fields. Those employed by manufacturing firms study methods of inventory control, for example, while those in banking study financial products offered by their bank. Data processing technicians also maintain a current and effective program library. These programs may be stored on magnetic tape, storage disks, or other machine-readable mediums. The programs are always subject to considerable revisions and modifications, and this requires maintaining careful records.

In specialized jobs in the scientific data processing field, the technician may spend time in other departments where the computer programs control the final work to be done. This adds variety to the data processing technician's work.

Business data processing technicians may work in the accounting department with the business methods planning, study, and control managers. There they help gather data or plan the collection, storage, and management of the data to provide the most needed and useful information for managing the business.

Requirements

High School

If you are interested in becoming a data processing technician, you should study accounting, business management, and computer technology. Most high schools offer at least an introductory course in computer programming. If you plan to be a business data processing technician, subjects such as accounting, inventory control, statistical methods, and similar business subjects are good.

Good language and communication skills can be developed in high school English and speech classes. An introductory-level course in drafting or engineering drawing taken in high school will be very useful to data processing technicians as well. Drawing, diagramming, and sketching are also helpful.

Postsecondary Training

There are many excellent educational institutions, both private and public, that offer two-year associate's degrees in computer-related technologies. If you want to become a data processing technician, you should follow courses of study that emphasize programming and software development. The curriculum for these degrees usually includes a number of specialized computer programming and systems concepts courses. Laboratory work, using the most modern equipment, is a vital part of students' education. Related courses in mathematics, statistics, accounting, business principles, economics, physics, engineering science, biology, or earth science also are required for graduation. Selection among these courses depends on your area of interest in either business or scientific data processing. Many institutions offer an associate's degree in both fields.

A two-year program in scientific data processing technology might begin with an orientation seminar followed by an introductory course on data processing. Courses might include technical mathematics, a science course (physics, electronics, chemistry, or biology), techniques of real-time and remote computation, statistics, statistical programming, life sciences, graphical representation, and technical reporting. The second year might include courses in fundamentals of scientific computation, Boolean algebra, linear programming, industrial organization and management, programming for engineering applications, scientific programming languages, introduction to operations research, a field project of the student's choosing, and general and industrial economics.

The two-year program in business data processing technology might begin with courses in communications skills, business machines, and technical mathematics. The first year would also include introduction to business, introduction to electronic data processing, business programming languages, business statistics, and principles of accounting. In the second year of business data processing, courses typically include economics, technical reporting, business management, systems and procedures, applied business systems, computer peripheral equipment and data storage systems, introduction to operations research, and computer language survey.

If you are seriously considering a career in this field, you should realize that your education will continue long after employment is secured. You will need to keep up with advances in technology, which constantly change the procedures, methods, equipment, and computer languages in use. Once employment is obtained, opportunities for further education are varied. Some companies and equipment manufacturers offer intensive seminars and workshops to keep employees and clients up to date on the latest technology. In some cases, technicians work with technology so new that formal training has yet to be developed. They may need to take supplementary evening or weekend courses to become qualified to work with the machines. The employer usually pays tuition and other costs of such job-related education.

Certification or Licensing

Although not mandatory, special certification is available for technicians who pass an examination administered by the Institute for Certification of Computing Professionals. This institute is sponsored by the Association of Information Technology Professionals (AITP), which started the program to encourage professional development within the field of data processing. One certification related to data processing is the Certified Computing Professional (CCP) designation. The examination for certification is offered in selected cities throughout the country each year. Even though the CCP certificate is not formally required by employers, it does provide favorable proof of accomplishment to employers when they hire or promote technicians. Contact information for AITP is given at the end of this article.

Other Requirements

The ability to think clearly and logically is the most important skill when working in a computer-related field. Data processing technicians enjoy the challenges of complex problem solving. They also need to communicate and work well with others. Because they often serve as communication channels between various people and the computer, they must be receptive to new ideas and be diplomatic in resolving misunderstandings among workers.

Exploring

If you are interested in data processing, you should ask your teachers and guidance counselors about specific courses offered by your school that might acquaint you with the work. Any form of computer experience is helpful, even computer games. Science or business courses and hobbies can lead to activities involving the use of computers to solve problems in science or business activities.

The local library or bookstore will undoubtedly have a selection of books and magazines on computers and computer programming. Becoming familiar with such material is excellent preparation for a career in the computer field. Similarly, joining a business or science club can open opportunities for you to become acquainted with and participate in activities that may lead to a technician career.

In addition to the traditional courses, you should read and study several professional journals and publications on computer technology. If possible, a career day visit to one or more businesses that employ data processing technicians or junior programmers would be helpful. Several computer user groups have formed professional organizations that offer opportunities for high school students to obtain information on educational and occupational requirements.

Employers

Data processing technicians are employed by larger companies and organizations that use computers to manage their day-to-day work. Some examples are businesses such as banks, manufacturers, and even specialized data processing centers.

Starting Out

Many students in a two-year data processing technical program find jobs before they graduate. This can be accomplished in several ways. One is through the school's placement office, which is responsible for maintaining a current file on local and national job openings. Classified advertisements and employment agencies can also be great sources of information concerning job openings.

Some industries and businesses send recruiters (usually personnel managers) to schools. Recruiters review applications and set up on-campus interviews with qualified students.

Graduates of two-year technical programs seeking entry-level data processing jobs may have to compete with many other job seekers. The great interest in the data processing and programming field in recent years has spurred the development of many training programs, including some that require a bachelor's degree. As the field matures and competition becomes tighter, a bachelor's degree will become more and more necessary for entry-level positions.

On-the-job training for the employer's specific data processing system is often necessary. A period of orientation at the beginning of the job, sometimes several months or even a year in length, may be required before the beginning technician is expected to have mastered the details of the employer's needs and processes.

In recent years, the trend toward computer-controlled automation in industries such as computer manufacturing and radio and television products has increased the need for scientific data processing technicians who know the industry. Many companies have met this need by sending their experienced electronic or electromechanical technicians to school to learn computer programming and data systems management. The same kind of program is also used to train other technical workers so that they can use the computer-controlled robots now being installed in some industries.

Advancement

Advancement opportunities for skilled data processing technicians are good. In addition to the steps from data processing technician to junior and senior programmer, there are parallel steps in supervision and management. Technicians who are considered extremely competent in the details of problem analysis and programming generally can progress to the analyst position. Advancement occurs faster for those whose education goes beyond a two-year technician program. Supervisory and managerial positions are available to technicians who show promise in managing and supervising people and projects.

As more companies become more heavily dependent on computers in their day-to-day operations, experienced technicians are finding increased opportunities to work as consultants. There are many companies and businesses that need help in designing custom systems using small computers, storage and information processing systems, and the programming know-how to apply computer technology to their work. Often, such a system and the ability to use it will make the difference between failure and success of a business.

In a similar way, data processing technicians and programming specialists in either numeric process control or computer graphics can often find excellent advancement opportunities working for consulting companies that specialize in these services.

Advancement is often a result of activities with and contacts in the many professional computer societies and organizations. The areas of concentration of such groups are diverse, ranging from systems management groups to special interest groups involved in research, statistical programming, and business programming.

Earnings

A data processing technician with an associate's degree in a computer-related technology can expect to earn between $18,000 and $22,000 per year to start. Technicians with experience and more programming responsibilities earn more—up to $30,000. From there, salaries increase depending on level of education attained and work experience. Top salaries for technicians reach about $33,000 per year. After that, technicians can be promoted to programming and analyst positions with higher pay.

The types of benefits available to data processing technicians will vary. Generally, paid vacations and holidays and some type of insurance program are provided. Many companies have a tuition reimbursement policy for employees who wish to further their education.

Many employers provide liberal opportunities for technicians and other data processing workers to study on the job or in school to keep the company up to date and competitive. Some employers also pay membership fees in scientific and technical societies.

Work Environment

Both scientific and business data processing technicians work in excellent environments. Computer equipment functions best in air-conditioned, dust-free office areas, so most technicians work in comfortable surroundings.

A technician's workweek usually does not exceed 40 hours. During computer emergencies and periods of heavy workloads, however, technicians may be required to work overtime. Some technicians may work on a shift basis if operations run 24 hours per day.

Part of a technician's work is completed independently of others. Otherwise, individual or group conferences with other programmers and information analysts are a regular part of the technician's work.

Outlook

Employment in the data processing field as a whole is expected to grow about as fast as the average for all occupations through the year 2006. Although demand for data processing technicians has decreased slightly, the prospects for growth are still favorable. This outlook is due to the great variety of computer applications constantly being devised.

As computers, software, and programming techniques are refined, many programming tasks become routine and automated or are eliminated altogether. This trend is slowing the growth in demand for personnel with two-year degrees in the data processing field. In addition, competition for jobs among graduates of technical programs is increasing as more beginning programmers enter the job market with four-year degrees. As a result, technicians with only two years of formal training may find relatively fewer satisfactory jobs open to them in the future.

For More Information

For information about careers in data processing and junior programming careers, contact:

Association of Information Technology Professionals
315 South Northwest Highway, Suite 200
Park Ridge, IL 60068
Tel: 847-825-8124
Email: 70430.35@compuserver.com
Web: http://www.aitp.org

For information on certification, contact:

Institute for Certification of Computing Professionals
2200 East Devon Avenue, Suite 247
Des Plaines, IL 60018
Tel: 800-843-8227
Email: 74040.3722@compuserve.com
Web: http://www.iccp.org

American Society for Information Science
8720 Georgia Avenue, Suite 501
Silver Spring, MD 20910-3602
Tel: 301-495-0900
Email: asis@asis.org
Web: http://www.asis.org

Database Design Analysts

Computer science Mathematics	School Subjects
Mechanical/manipulative Technical/scientific	Personal Skills
Primarily indoors Primarily one location	Work Environment
Bachelor's degree	Minimum Education Level
$35,000 to $50,000 to $70,000+	Salary Range
None available	Certification or Licensing
Faster than the average	Outlook

Overview

Database design analysts, evaluate the needs of a business, map out a database structure that will meet those needs, and design program specifications for programmers and database administrators. Database design requires analysts to pay careful attention to many variables at the once. They also make sound decisions about the usefulness of certain system features, considering the trade-off between the added features and the increased cost.

History

The first major advances in modern computer technology were made during World War II. After the war, people thought that computers were too big (they easily filled entire warehouses) to ever be used for anything other than government projects, such as processing the census.

The introduction of semiconductors to computer technology made possible smaller and less-expensive computers. The semiconductors replaced the bigger, slower vacuum tubes of the first computers. These changes made it easier for businesses to adapt computers to their needs, which they began doing as early as 1954. Within 30 years, computers had revolutionized the way people work, play, and even shop. Today, computers are everywhere, from businesses of all kinds, to government agencies, charitable organizations, and private homes. Over the years, technology has continued to shrink computer size and increase computer speed at an unprecedented rate.

Technological advances have made database computing a subfield of tremendous growth and potential. Businesses and other organizations not only use databases to replace existing paper-based procedures but also create new uses for them every day. For example, catalog companies use databases to organize inventory and sales systems, which they previously did by hand. These same companies are pushing technology further by investigating ways to use databases to customize promotional materials. Instead of sending the same catalog out to everyone, some companies want to send each customer a special edition filled with items he or she would be sure to like, based on past purchases and a personal profile.

Database design analysts are crucial participants in database development. In fact, many companies who took an inexpensive route to database computing by constructing databases haphazardly are now sorry they did not initially hire a design analyst. Design work is important because it translates difficult, abstract relationships into concrete, logical structures. If the work is done well to begin with, the database will be better suited to handle changes in the future.

Most commercial computer systems make use of some kind of database. As computer speed and memory capacity continue to increase, more database uses will be created. Therefore, database design analysts will enjoy good job prospects for years to come.

The Job

In the past, most companies maintained huge storage rooms filled with filing cabinets brimming with hard copy records. Now, most firms have input all important data into computer systems, since they are easier and more efficient to operate. Businesses use computers to store huge amounts of information. They maintain employee data, client profiles, sales records, and many other types of files on computers. Just as every business used to rely on a well-organized filing system to make retrieval and modification of records easy, businesses require the same kind of well-planned organization system for their computerized records.

The program that structures how information is stored, how separate pieces of information relate and affect one another, and how the overall system should be organized is called a *database*. For example, a business's customer database will have a separate "record" for each customer, in the same way that each customer formerly had a separate file folder in a file cabinet. In the business's sales database, each sale represented by an invoice will have a separate record. Each record contains many "fields" where specific pieces of information are entered. Examples of fields for the customer database include Customer number, Customer name, Address, City, State, Zip code, Phone, and Contact person. Examples of fields in the sales database include Customer number, Item purchased, Quantity, Price, Date of purchase, and Total. With information organized in this way, in separate fields, the business can easily sort (the equivalent to filing file folders in the file cabinet) its customer records or invoices any way it wants. It could print a list of all customers in Iowa, for example, or total sales for the month of April. In the same way that records within a database can be sorted, databases themselves can be related to each other. The customer database can be related to the sales database by the common field, Customer number. Therefore, the business could print out a list of all purchases by a specific customer, for example, or a list of customers who purchased a specific product.

Other duties might include providing technical support for existing databases; modifying existing databases as circumstances change; and customizing commercial databases for specific needs. Database specialists also plan and design databases for new clients, which includes solving problems to meet those clients' needs. Specialists might program databases for a variety of applications and oversee the installation of new databases. Database specialists might also train staff members in client companies about using new or existing databases.

Requirements

High School

If you are still in high school, take as many math, science, and computer classes as you can. These courses provide the basics as well as encourage rigorous logical thinking. You should also take English and philosophy classes since these subjects promote good communications and analytical thinking skills. Any courses that rely on schematic drawings and technical writing can be good preparation for postsecondary course work in computer science.

Postsecondary Training

A bachelor's degree in computer science or another computer-related discipline is usually a minimum requirement for individuals wishing to become database design analysts. Some exceptions are made for people who have extensive experience in database administration and who have trained in the field. As the job market matures, more and more database professionals will be college educated. Therefore, you should plan on pursuing postsecondary education.

Other Requirements

Database design analysts are strong logical and analytical thinkers. They excel at analyzing massive amounts of information and organizing it into a coherent structure composed of complicated relationships. They are also good at weighing the importance of each element of a system and deciding which ones can be omitted without diminishing the quality of the final project. They are good at analyzing projects from a general and detailed perspective and, to use a common expression, they can see the "forest" and the "trees" simultaneously.

Database design analysts should also have strong communications skills. The work requires contact with employees from a wide variety of jobs. Design analysts must be able to ask clear, concise, and technical questions of people who are not necessarily familiar with how databases work.

As is true for all other computer professionals, design analysts should be motivated to keep up with technological advances and be able to learn new things very quickly. A solid understanding of computer basics, both hardware and software, is fundamental to ongoing success in this field.

Exploring

If you are interested in this field, participate in school-sponsored career days, spending a day on the job with a design analyst if possible. Such visits can also be arranged individually with certain companies and are a good way to experience firsthand what a typical day is like.

Playing strategy games with friends is another good activity. These games are available in a variety of topics, from war simulations to world history and development. They offer an opportunity for you to put your analytical thinking skills to use in a fun environment. The key is to practice the kinds of skills that are used in design work, as described above.

Most important, learn everything you can about computers by working with them regularly. Online sources can be particularly good for keeping up to date with new developments and learning from people who are actively involved in this type of work. Learning a commercial database program, either by teaching yourself or by attending a special class, is basic. Offer to set up small databases, such as address books, recipe databases, or videotape libraries for friends or family members to accommodate their needs. You might also try computer programming in conjunction with school projects.

"Start by reading books on the subject," says Scott Sciaretta, an internal database consultant for Choicepoint Inc. in Atlanta, Georgia. "There are hundreds of them at most bookstores. Try to get a job as an intern in a database shop and learn by watching, mentoring, and grunt work."

Employers

Any business or company that uses databases as a part of its operations hires database professionals. These include retail stores, catalog companies, insurance companies, communications services, financial institutions, hospitals, government agencies, schools, computer companies, universities, and businesses in service industries.

Starting Out

Most database design analyst positions are obtained in one of two ways—either a lower-level database specialist is promoted or a new college graduate is hired. Working computer professionals should be aware of openings in their companies as they become available. They should also actively seek the extra training or formal education required for design jobs in their firms. If they wish to change companies, they can work with headhunters and employment agencies. In this case, a college degree is more important since the prospective employer does not have direct knowledge of an individual's experience and performance to guide hiring decisions.

College students should work closely with their schools' placement offices. Local and national employers often recruit college graduates on campus, making it much easier for students to talk with many diverse companies. Also, students should try to obtain meaningful summer internships related to their fields of interest. Many major computer companies, such as Apple, Intel, Oracle, and Netscape, have established undergraduate intern programs. Experience in such programs is valuable for two reasons. First, it gives students hands-on exposure to computer-related jobs. Second, it allows students to network with working computer professionals who may help them find full-time jobs upon graduation.

Another job-hunting method is Career Mosaic on the World Wide Web. This service provides easy access to hundreds of job openings posted on the Internet.

Advancement

Database design analysts hold high positions within database departments. Therefore, advancement is highly dependent on the interests of each individual. Generally, people fall into two categories—those who want to work in management and those who prefer to stay in technical jobs. For individuals who want to get into the managerial side of the business, formal education in business administration is usually required. The educational requirement can sometimes be waived, however, when a design analyst seeks promotion within his or her own company. Still, upper-level management positions are reserved for college graduates with a bachelor's or master's degree in business or business administration. Design analysts who demonstrate talent in organization, interpersonal communication, and formal presentations as well as long-term vision for the company can be offered promotion into management. Most computing managers have a solid and diverse background in computer technology. But technical expertise is not enough. As managers, they must work on cross-functional teams with professionals in finance, sales, personnel, purchasing, and operations. They must be able to determine how decisions made in their department affect the other areas of the business.

Some database design analysts prefer to stay on the technical side of the business. For them, the hands-on computer work is the best part of their job. The thought of managing people and budgets instead of setting up computer systems does not excite them. Since design analysis is one of the highest levels within database systems, individuals often look to other areas of computing for promotion. Systems analysis, software design, and networking are possible options. A move into one of these jobs carries the extra benefit of broadening technical expertise. Database design analysts should pursue training and education in the area of interest before seeking promotion. Becoming a freelance database design consultant is another option for the experienced analyst.

"I got my first job in the field by internal promotion," says Scott. "Basically, I was doing some computer programming for my department on the side to automate a few of the menial tasks. My work got noticed, and I was given the job of running the company's computer department when the position opened. At my current level, the advancement opportunities are not easy. For me to advance I either need to expand my scope or work for a larger company, both of which are very feasible with hard work. However, salary advancements are easy and can be quite large. There are many opportunities for advancement for entry-level or junior positions."

Earnings

Beginning database design analysts with a college education can expect to earn about $35,000 per year to start. This figure varies depending on the precise level of the job, quality of education, and related experience, if any, of the applicant. Mid-level salaries, offered to professionals with several years of experience, average about $50,000. After more experience and further training, database design analysts earn top salaries of $70,000. However, some individuals earn even more depending on their employer and the size of the projects for which they are responsible. Most full-time database design analysts work for companies that offer the full range of benefits, including health insurance, sick leave, and paid vacation.

Database design analysts who work as independent consultants usually make between $55 and $65 an hour. Typically, only professionals with experience and a broad range of business contacts work in this capacity.

Work Environment

Database design analysts work primarily indoors in a comfortable office environment. If they work as consultants, they may travel to client sites as little as once or twice per project or as often as every week. Travel requirements vary with employer, client, and level of position held. Design analysts typically have a lot of meetings to attend, especially during the planning stages of a project. They work regular 40-hour weeks but may put in overtime as deadlines approach. During these crunch times, the work can be quite stressful since accuracy and completeness are very important. Design analysts must therefore be able to work well under pressure and respond quickly to last-minute changes. Some design analysts experience frustration when clients change the parameters of a project as time goes on. As explained above, the careful mapping out of the database is crucial for success. If the rules change in midstream, many characteristics of the database may change, too. Design analysts are expected to visualize far-reaching implications of such changes and respond accordingly.

"I like what I do. It's kind of like playing," Scott says. "The hours are flexible. You get to work on and set up million-dollar systems. There also is a high degree of visibility from upper management. The downside is that I work lots of hours, including many weekends, and I have a never-ending list of work. The hardest part of the job is juggling the schedules and configurations for many projects at one time."

Outlook

Employment in database design analysis is expected to grow faster than the average for all other occupations through 2006, according to the U.S. Department of Labor. One major reason is the increasing demand for database design by major computer users. Computer companies and consulting firms will hire design analysts to complete such projects. Also, firms in industries such as manufacturing, insurance, and banking will hire in-house database experts to work on their systems.

Interested students should stay up to date on advances in database technology as the development of certain back-end systems and front-end applications may alter the specific responsibilities of design analysts. For example, database coding tools may eliminate the need for design analysts to do any coding at all. However, the analytical aspects of design work (mapping out the system) are likely to remain a human task, even if more helping tools are created.

"The field of Unix systems and databases is wide open," notes Scott. "There is and will be greater demand for good talent than the industry can supply. I would recommend a database administration field. Most companies are moving to larger databases, and the need for particularly Oracle and Microsoft SQL Server database administrators is a bottomless pit."

For More Information

For information on scholarships, student membership, and the student newsletter, looking.forward, *contact:*

IEEE Computer Society
1730 Massachusetts Avenue, NW
Washington, DC 20036-1992
Tel: 202-371-0101
Web: http://www.computer.org

Database Specialists

Computer science Mathematics	School Subjects
Mechanical/manipulative Technical/scientific	Personal Skills
Primarily indoors Primarily one location	Work Environment
Associate's degree	Minimum Education Level
$17,000 to $54,000 to $67,500+	Salary Range
Voluntary	Certification or Licensing
Much faster than the average	Outlook

Overview

Database specialists design, install, update, modify, maintain, and repair computer database systems. They consult with other management officials to discuss computer equipment purchases, determine requirements for various computer programs, and allocate access to the computer system to users. They might also direct training of personnel who use company databases regularly. There are over 212,000 database specialists employed in the United States.

History

Computers play a large role in all aspects of our lives. Nowhere is this fact more apparent than in the private and government sectors, where computers are being put to use in a rapidly growing range of business, military, and educational situations. Developments in electronics have made it possible to build miniature digital computers, minicomputers, and microprocessors. Integrated circuits have made low-cost, high-speed computer systems available to many businesses and other organizations that previously could not afford them.

We are now firmly rooted in an era referred to as the "Information Age." Vast amounts of information about people, places, and events are recorded electronically in the form of databases. Whereas just 10 or 20 years ago the transfer of information from one company to another could be slow and cumbersome, computers now routinely exchange information rapidly via telephone lines and networks 24 hours a day. This explosive growth in the computer field has led to increasingly large and complex databases. The individuals and businesses that specialize in inputting, organizing, and making available various types of information stand at the forefront of an ever-growing field.

The Job

Database specialists come in many varieties, depending on the needs of the organizations that employ them. In large businesses there may be several database specialists who focus on specific aspects of a company's databases. In a smaller organization, one person may wear all the database hats. Database specialists are also known as *database administrators, database managers,* or *information systems managers.* Database specialists rely on their knowledge of database management to code, test, and install new databases. They review proposals for changes in existing database systems and evaluate how well such changes would work on a daily basis. They are also responsible for overseeing the daily operations of the computer systems. These tasks include ensuring that information is being entered and encoded properly by data entry clerks, that various processing programs are retrieving the right information, and that the systems are not experiencing major problems.

Database specialists are responsible for the flow of computer information within an organization. They make major decisions concerning computer purchases, system designs, and personnel training. Their duties combine general management ability with a detailed knowledge of computer programming and systems analysis.

The specific responsibilities of a database specialist are determined by the size and type of employer. For example, a database manager for a telephone company may develop a system for billing customers, while a database manager for a large store may develop a system for keeping track of merchandise in stock. In all cases, most database specialists have a thorough knowledge and understanding of the company's computer operations.

A database specialist's responsibilities can be grouped into three main areas: planning the type of computer system a company needs; implementing and managing the system; and supervising computer room personnel.

To adequately plan a computer system, database specialists must have extensive knowledge of the latest computer technology and the specific needs of their company. Database specialists meet with other high-ranking company officials, such as the president or vice president, and together they decide how to apply the available technology to their company's needs. Decisions include what type of hardware and software to order and how the data should be stored. Database specialists must be aware of the cost of the proposed computer system as well as the budget within which the company is operating. Long-term planning is also important. Database managers must ensure that the computer system can process not only the existing level of computer information received but also the anticipated load and type of information the company could receive in the future. Such planning is vitally important since, even for small companies, computer systems can cost several hundred thousand dollars.

Database managers must be familiar with accounting principles and mathematical formulas in developing proposals. It is not unusual for a database manager to modify an existing computer system or develop a whole new system based on a company's needs and resources.

Implementing and managing a computer system entails a variety of administrative tasks. Database administrators decide how to organize and store the information files so only the appropriate users gain access to them. In addition, program files must be coded for efficient retrieval. Scheduling access to the computer is another vital administrative function. Sometimes, database administrators work with representatives from all departments to create a schedule. The administrator prioritizes needs and monitors usage so that each department can do its work. All computer usage must be documented and filed away for future reference.

Safeguarding the computer operations is another important responsibility of database specialists. They must make plans in case a computer system fails or malfunctions so that the information stored in the computer is not lost. A duplication of computer files may be a part of this emergency planning. A backup system must also be employed so that the company can continue to process information. Increasingly, database specialists must also safeguard a system so that only authorized personnel have access to certain information. Computerized information may be of vital importance to a company, and database specialists ensure that it does not fall into the wrong hands.

Implementation of a computer operation often involves coordinating the integration of many complex computers into a single system. As an operation grows, this may require the modification of the system.

Database managers must be able to analyze a computer operation and decide if it is operating at top efficiency. They must be able to recognize equipment or personnel problems and adjust the system accordingly. They are often working with an operation that processes millions of bits of information at a huge cost. This demands accuracy and efficiency in decision-making and problem-solving abilities.

Requirements

High School

Prior experience with computers is essential to obtaining a position as a database specialist. If you are interested in this field you should take computer programming courses and any electronics or other technical courses that provide understanding of how a computer operates. Mathematics, science, and accounting courses are also desirable. English and speech courses are a good way for you to hone your written and verbal communications skills.

Postsecondary Training

A bachelor's degree is often a prerequisite to be hired as a computer professional. Sometimes, if the candidate shows exceptional experience in the computer field, an associate's degree in a computer-related technology from a technical or vocational school is sufficient to fulfill education requirements. Course work may include classes in electronics, computer hardware and software, physics, mathematics, schematic reading, and basic programming. Many employers prefer their database administrators to have a background in computer science, information science, computer information systems, or data processing.

Promotion from entry-level administrator jobs to managerial positions will require a bachelor's degree in one of the following: computer science, information science, computer information systems, data processing, or business administration. Sometimes, work experience within the company can compensate for a lack of more formal education. Courses in a bachelor's degree program usually include data processing, systems analysis methods, more detailed software and hardware concepts, management principles, and information systems planning. Many businesses, especially larger companies, prefer database managers to have a master's degree in computer science or business administration.

Certification or Licensing

Some database specialists become certified for jobs in the computer field by passing an examination given by the Institute for Certification of Computing Professionals (ICCP). The examination is offered in selected cities throughout the United States every year. For further information on certification, contact the ICCP at the address given at the end of this article.

Other Requirements

Experience as a computer programmer or systems analyst is also desirable. Those familiar with programming languages will be in demand. Individuals interested in working almost exclusively in one industry, such as banking, for example, should acquire as much knowledge as possible about that specific field in addition to their extensive computer training. General knowledge in database administration might not prepare an individual for working in a bank unless he or she also understands basic bank operations and goals. With an understanding of both fields, individuals are more easily able to apply computer technology to the specific needs of the company.

Exploring

High school computer clubs offer a good forum for learning about computers and meeting others interested in the field. Some businesses offer part-time work or summer internships in their computer departments for qualified students. In addition, there are training programs, such as those offered at summer camps, that teach computer literacy during an intensive three- to six-week period. You might also ask your school administrators about databases used by the school and try to interview any database specialists working in or for the school system. Similar attempts could be made with charities in your local area that make use of computer databases for membership and client records as well as mailing lists.

Employers

Database specialists work for investment companies, telecommunications firms, banks, insurance companies, publishing houses, and a host of other large and midsize businesses and nonprofit organizations. There are also many opportunities with the federal, state, and city governments. Teaching, whether as a consultant or at a university or community college, is another option for individuals with high levels of experience.

Starting Out

Since at least an associate's degree is needed to obtain a position in this field, most database professionals work closely with their schools' placement offices to obtain information about job openings and interviews. Interested individuals might also scan the classified ads or work with temporary agencies to find entry-level and midlevel positions. Some applicants with extensive on-the-job computer training may be promoted to this position without a degree, but as the field gets more sophisticated, a college degree will continue to be the most dependable means of entering the profession.

College internships or co-op programs are good ways to gain credible work experience and meet valuable contacts for the future. Many businesses favor applicants already familiar with company standards and goals.

Advancement

Skilled database specialists have excellent advancement opportunities. As specialists acquire education and develop solid work experience, advancement will take the form of more responsibilities and higher wages. Database administrators may bepromoted into database design and management positions. A database specialist at a small company that relies heavily on database technology might move to an upper-level position, such as vice president of the firm or might move to a better-paying, more challenging database position at a larger company. Superior database managers at larger companies may also be promoted to executive positions. Some successful database managers become highly paid consultants or start their own businesses.

Earnings

Earnings vary with the size and type of organization and a person's experience, education, and job responsibilities. A database administrator with an associate's degree can earn around $17,000 per year. According to Robert Half International, Inc., those with a bachelor's degree earned between $54,000 and $67,500 a year in 1997. However, database administrators, depending on the company and the degree of responsibility, could easily earn more. Consultants working for major computer companies usually earn higher salaries.

Work Environment

Database specialists work in modern offices, usually located next to computer rooms. Most duties are performed at a computer on the individual's desk. Travel is occasionally required for conferences and visits to affiliated database locations.

Database specialists work a regular 40-hour week, but higher-level positions sometimes require longer hours, especially when major system changes are being implemented. Emergencies may also require specialists to work overtime or long hours without a break, sometimes through the night.

Outlook

The use of computers and database systems in almost all business creates tremendous opportunities for well-qualified database personnel. Database specialists and computer support specialists are predicted by the U.S. Department of Labor to be the two fastest growing occupations through the year 2006. In 1996, there were 212,000 database specialists employed in the United States. By the year 2006, the U.S. Department of Labor expects about 250,000 new jobs in this field—a 115 percent increase. Those with the best education and the most experience in computer systems and personnel management will find the best job prospects.

Employment opportunities for database specialists should be best in large urban areas because of the multitudes of businesses that have computer systems. Since smaller communities are also rapidly developing significant job opportunities, skilled workers can pick from a wide range of jobs throughout the country.

For More Information

For general information on career opportunities or information regarding one of their 300 student chapters, contact:

Association of Information Technology Professionals
315 South Northwest Highway, Suite 200
Park Ridge, IL 60068-4278
Tel: 800-224-9371
Email: 70430.35@compuserve.com
Web: http://www.aitp.org

For more information about computer certification, contact:

Institute for Certification of Computing Professionals
2200 East Devon Avenue, Suite 247
Des Plaines, IL 60018
Tel: 847-299-4227
Email: 74040.3722@compuserve.com
Web: http://www.iccp.org

Graphic Designers

Art Computer science	School Subjects
Artistic Communication/ideas	Personal Skills
Primarily indoors Primarily one location	Work Environment
Some postsecondary training	Minimum Education Level
$23,000 to $50,000 to $85,000+	Salary Range
None available	Certification or Licensing
Faster than the average	Outlook

Overview

Graphic designers are practical artists whose creations are intended to express ideas, convey information, or draw attention to a product. They design a wide variety of materials including advertisements, displays, packaging, signs, computer graphics and games, book and magazine covers and interiors, animated characters, and company logos to fit the needs and preferences of their various clients.

History

The challenge of combining beauty, function, and technology in whatever form has preoccupied artisans in all periods of history. Graphic design work has been used to create products and promote commerce for as long as people have used symbols, pictures, and typography to communicate ideas.

Graphic design work grew with the growth of print media—newspapers, magazines, catalogs, and advertising. Typically, the graphic designer would sketch several rough drafts of the layout of pictures and words. After one of the drafts was approved, the designer would complete a final layout including detailed type and artwork specifications. The words were sent to a typesetter and the artwork was assigned to an illustrator. When the final pieces were returned, the designer or a keyline and paste-up artist would adhere them with rubber cement or wax to an illustration board. Different colored items were placed on acetate overlays. This camera-ready art was now ready to be sent to a printer for photographing and reproduction.

Computer technology has revolutionized the way many graphic designers do their work: today it is possible to be a successful graphic designer even if you can't draw more than simple stick figures. Graphic designers are now able to draw, color, and revise the many different images they work with daily. They can choose typefaces, size type, and place it without having to align it on the page using a T-square and triangle. Computer graphics enable graphic designers to work more quickly since details like size, shape, and color are easy to change.

Graphics programs for computers are continually revised and improved, moving more and more design work from the artist's table to the computer mousepad and graphics tablet. This area of computer technology is booming now and will be in the future, as computer graphics and multimedia move toward virtual reality applications. Many graphic designers with solid computer experience will be needed to work with these systems.

The Job

Graphic designers are not primarily fine artists, although they may be highly skilled at drawing or painting. Most designs commissioned to graphic designers involve both artwork and copy (that is, words). Thus, the designer must not only be familiar with the wide range of art media (photography, drawing, painting, collage, etc.) and styles, but he or she must also be familiar with a wide range of typefaces and know how to manipulate them for the right effect. Because design tends to change like fashion, designers must keep up to date with the latest trends. At the same time, they must be well-grounded in more traditional, classic designs.

Graphic designers can work as in-house designers for a particular company, as staff designers for a graphic design firm, or as freelance designers working for themselves. Some designers specialize in designing advertising materials or packaging. Others focus on corporate identity materials, such as company stationery and logos. Some work mainly for publishers designing book and magazine covers and page layouts. Some work in the area of computer graphics, creating still or animated graphics for computer software, videos, or motion pictures. A highly specialized type of graphic designer, the *environmental graphic designer,* designs large outdoor signs. Some graphic designers design exclusively on the computer, while others may use both the computer and traditional hand drawings or paintings, depending on the project's needs and requirements.

Whatever the specialty and whatever their medium, all graphic designers take a similar approach to a project, whether it is for an entirely new design or for a variation on an existing one. Graphic designers begin by determining as best they can the needs and preferences of the clients and the potential users, buyers, or viewers.

In the case of a graphic designer working on a company logo, for example, he or she is likely to meet with company representatives to discuss such points as how and where the company is going to use the logo and what size, color, and shape preferences company executives might have. Project budgets must be carefully respected: a design that may be perfect in every way but that is too costly to reproduce is basically useless. Graphic designers may need to compare their ideas with similar ones from other companies and analyze the image they project. Thus they must have a good knowledge of how various colors, shapes, and layouts affect the viewer psychologically.

After a plan has been conceived and the details worked out, the graphic designer does some preliminary designs (generally two or three) to present to the client for approval. The client may reject the preliminary design entirely and request a new design, or he or she may ask the designer to make alterations to the existing design. The designer then goes back to the drawing board to attempt a new design or make the requested changes. This process continues until the client approves the design.

Once a design has been approved, the graphic designer prepares the design for professional reproduction, that is, printing. The printer may require a "mechanical," in which the artwork and copy are arranged on a white board just as it is to be photographed, or the designer may be asked to submit an electronic copy of the design. Either way, designers must have a good understanding of the printing process, including color separation, paper properties, and *halftone* (i.e., photograph) reproduction.

Requirements

High School

High school students should take any art and design courses that are available. Computer classes are also helpful, particularly those that teach page layout programs or art and photography manipulation programs. Working on the school newspaper or yearbook can provide valuable design experience. You may also volunteer to design flyers or posters for school events.

Postsecondary Training

More graphic designers are recognizing the value of formal training, and at least two out of three people entering the field today have a college degree or some college education. Over one hundred colleges and art schools offer graphic design programs that are accredited by the National Association of Schools of Art and Design. At many schools, graphic design students must take a year of basic art and design courses before being accepted into the bachelor's degree program. In addition, applicants to the bachelor's degree programs in graphic arts may be asked to submit samples of their work to prove artistic ability. Many schools and employers depend on samples, or portfolios, to evaluate the applicants' skills in graphic design.

Many programs increasingly emphasize the importance of using computers for design work. Computer proficiency among graphic designers will be very important in the years to come. Interested individuals should select an academic program that incorporates computer training into the curriculum, or train themselves on their own.

A bachelor of fine arts program at a four-year college or university may include courses such as principles of design, art and art history, painting, sculpture, mechanical and architectural drawing, architecture, computerized design, basic engineering, fashion designing and sketching, garment construction, and textiles. Such degrees are desirable but not always necessary for obtaining a position as a graphic designer.

Other Requirements

Like all other artists, graphic designers need a degree of artistic talent, creativity, and imagination. They must be sensitive to beauty and have an eye for detail and a strong sense of color, balance, and proportion. To a great extent, these qualities are natural, but they can be developed through training, both on the job and in professional schools, colleges, and universities.

More and more, graphic designers need solid computer skills and working knowledge of several of the common drawing, image editing, and page layout programs. Graphic design on the computer is done on both Macintosh systems and on PC systems; many designers have both types of computers in their studios.

With or without specialized education, graphic designers seeking employment should have a good portfolio containing samples of their best work. The graphic designer's portfolio is extremely important and can make a difference when an employer must choose between two otherwise equally qualified candidates.

A period of on-the-job training is expected for all beginning designers. The length of time it takes to become fully qualified as a graphic designer may run from one to three years, depending on prior education and experience as well as innate talent.

Exploring

High school students interested in a career in graphic design have a number of ways to find out whether they have the talent, ambition, and perseverance to succeed in the field. Students should take as many art and design courses as possible while still in high school and should become proficient at working on computers. In addition, to get an insider's view of various design occupations, they could enlist the help of art teachers or school guidance counselors to make arrangements to tour design companies and interview designers.

While studying, students interested in graphic design can get practical experience by participating in school and community projects that call for design talents. These might include such activities as building sets for plays, setting up exhibits, planning seasonal and holiday displays, and preparing programs and other printed materials. For those interested in publication design, work on the school newspaper or yearbook is invaluable.

Part-time and summer jobs offer would-be designers an excellent way to become familiar with the day-to-day requirements of a particular design occupation and to gain some basic related experience. Possible places of employment include design studios, design departments in advertising agencies and manufacturing companies, department and furniture stores, flower shops, workshops that produce ornamental items, and museums. Museums also use a number of volunteer workers. Inexperienced people are often employed as sales, clerical, or general helpers; those with a little more education and experience may qualify for jobs in which they have a chance to develop actual design skills and to build portfolios of completed design projects.

Employers

Graphic designers work in many different industries, including the wholesale and retail trade (department stores, furniture and home furnishings stores, apparel stores, florist shops); manufacturing industries (machinery, motor vehicles and aircraft, metal products, instruments, apparel, textiles, printing and publishing); service industries (business services, engineering, architecture); construction firms; and government agencies. Public relations and publicity firms, advertising agencies, commercial printers, and mail-order houses all have graphic design departments. The publishing industry is a primary employer of graphic designers, including book publishers, magazines, newspapers, and newsletters. Many graphic designers are self-employed and hire their freelance services to multiple clients.

Starting Out

The best way to enter the field of graphic design is to have a strong portfolio. Potential employers rely on portfolios to evaluate talent and how that talent might be used to fit the company's special needs. Beginning graphic designers can assemble a portfolio from work completed at school, in art classes, and in part-time or freelance jobs. The portfolio should continually be updated to reflect the designer's growing skills so it will always be ready for possible job changes.

Job interviews may be obtained by applying directly to companies that employ designers. Many colleges and professional schools have placement services to help their graduates find positions. Sometimes they can get referral from a previous part-time employer or volunteer coordinator.

Advancement

As part of their on-the-job training, beginning graphic designers generally are given the simpler tasks and work under direct supervision. As they gain experience, they move up to more complex work with increasingly less supervision.

Experienced graphic designers, especially those with leadership capabilities, may be promoted to chief designer, design department head, or other supervisory positions.

Computer graphic designers can move into other computer-related positions with additional education. Some may become interested in graphics programming in order to further improve computer design capabilities. Others may want to become involved with multimedia and interactive graphics. Video games, touch-screen displays in stores, and even laser light shows are all products of multimedia graphic designers.

When designers develop personal styles that are in high demand in the marketplace, they sometimes go into business for themselves. Freelance design work can be erratic, however, so usually only the most experienced designers with an established client base can count on consistent full-time work.

Earnings

The range of salaries for graphic designers is quite broad. Many earn as little as $17,000, while others receive more than $35,000. Salaries depend primarily on the nature and scope of the employer, with computer graphic designers earning wages on the high end of the range.

Self-employed designers can earn a lot one year and substantially more or less the next. Their earnings depend on individual talent and business ability, but, in general, are higher than those of salaried designers, although like any self-employed individual, they must pay their own insurance costs and taxes and are not compensated for vacation or sick days.

The Society of Publication Designers has estimated that entry-level graphic designers earned between $23,000 and $27,000 annually in 1997. Salaried designers who advance to the position of design manager or design director earn about $60,000 a year and, at the level of corporate vice-president, make $70,000 and up. The owner of a consulting firm can make $85,000 or more.

Graphic designers who work for large corporations receive full benefits, including health insurance, paid vacation, and sick leave.

Work Environment

Most graphic designers work regular hours in clean, comfortable, pleasant offices or studios. Conditions vary depending on the design specialty.

Some graphic designers work in small establishments with few employees; others, in large organizations with large design departments. Some deal mostly with their co-workers; others may have a lot of public contact. Freelance designers are paid by the assignment. To maintain a steady income, they must constantly strive to please their clients and to find new ones.

Computer graphic designers may have to work long, irregular hours in order to complete an especially ambitious project.

Outlook

Chances for employment look very good for qualified graphic designers through the year 2006, especially for those involved with computer graphics. The design field in general is expected to grow at a faster than average rate. As computer graphic technology continues to advance, there will be a need for well-trained computer graphic designers. Companies that have always used graphics will expect their designers to perform work on computers. Companies for which graphic design was once too time-consuming or costly are now sprucing up company newsletters and magazines, among other things, and need graphic designers to do it.

Because the design field is a popular one, appealing to many talented individuals, competition is expected to be strong in all areas. Beginners and designers with only average talent or without formal education and technical skills may encounter some difficulty in securing employment.

About one-third of all graphic designers are self-employed, a higher proportion than is found in most other occupations.

For More Information

American Center for Design
233 East Ontario, Suite 500
Chicago, IL 60611
Tel: 312-787-2018

For more information about careers in graphic design, contact:

American Institute of Graphic Arts
164 Fifth Avenue
New York, NY 10160-1652
Tel: 800-548-1634
Web: http://www.aiga.org

National Association of Schools of Art and Design
11250 Roger Bacon Drive, Suite 21
Reston, VA 22090
Tel: 703-437-0700

Society for Environmental Graphic Design
1 Story Street
Cambridge, MA 02138
Tel: 617-868-3381

Society of Publication Designers
60 East 42nd Street, Suite 721
New York, NY 10165
Tel: 212-983-8585

Urban Art International
PO Box 868
Tiburon, CA 94920
Tel: 415-435-5767
Web: http://www.imagesite.com

Graphics Programmers

	School Subjects
Art Computer science	

	Personal Skills
Artistic Technical/scientific	

	Work Environment
Primarily indoors Primarily one location	

	Minimum Education Level
Bachelor's degree	

	Salary Range
$35,000 to $50,000 to $68,000+	

	Certification or Licensing
None available	

	Outlook
Faster than the average	

Overview

Graphics programmers design software that allows computers to generate graphic designs, charts, and illustrations for manufacturing, communications, entertainment, and engineering. They also develop computer applications that graphic designers use to create multimedia presentations, posters, logos, layouts for publication, and many other objects.

History

Developed from technology used during World War II, the first modern computer was used in 1951 to organize the population data compiled in the 1950 U.S. Census. At that time, computers were considered nothing more than electronic systems for storing and retrieving information. Because of their immense size and development costs, plus the difficulty of installing and programming them, it was thought that computers would only be useful for huge projects such as a nationwide census. But private companies were quick to explore ways to harness the power of the computer to gain an edge over their competitors. Today, computer technology has been adapted for use in practically every field and industry, from manufacturing to medicine, from telephones to space exploration, from engineering to entertainment and art.

Computers are not only used to store and organize data; they also communicate data to other computers and to users. Computer scientists have made great strides in adapting computer technology for visual presentation. Graphics are important communications tools and are now used in many diverse industries to interpret and display the relationships between various data elements. They can be used to illustrate difficult or abstract concepts, show ratios and proportions, or demonstrate how forces such as the weather change over time. As the graphics field has expanded, the emphasis has shifted from two-dimensional solutions, such as brochures or posters, to three-dimensional design, including screen displays for television and World Wide Web pages, according to the Computer Museum. Computer graphics can also be used for interactive automobile design, medical simulations, real-estate home walk-throughs, animation, flight simulations, digital movie special effects, and virtual reality.

Although "hand skills," such as drawing and drafting are still used occasionally in graphics design, the computer has become the primary tool. The advantages of using computers are many, including speed, precision, and on-screen editing.

The Job

The graphics programmer's job is similar to that of other computer programmers—determining what the computer will be expected to do and writing instructions for the computer that will allow it to carry out these functions. For a computer to perform any operation at all, detailed instructions must be written into its memory in a computer language, such as BASIC, COBOL, PASCAL, C, C++, or Virtual Reality Markup Language (VRML). The programmer is responsible for telling the computer exactly what to do.

The details involved in a graphics programmer's job can be illustrated by tracing how a graphics program designed for desktop publishing is developed. Working with a computer systems analyst, the graphics programmer's first step is to interview managers or clients to determine the kinds of tasks the program will be expected to perform, such as drawing shapes, organizing text, and adding different colors. The programmer investigates current computer graphics capabilities and how to improve them.

Once the expectations of the program are identified, the programmer usually prepares a flowchart, which illustrates on paper how the computer will process the incoming information and carry out its operations. The programmer then begins to write the instructions for the computer in a language, such as C or C++. The coded instructions will also contain comments so other programmers can understand it.

Once the program is written, it is tested thoroughly by programmers, graphic designers, and quality assurance testers to make sure it can do the desired tasks. The programmer reviews the results of the tests to see where any problems lie. If problems, or glitches, do exist, the program must be altered and retested until it produces the correct results. This is known as *debugging* the program.

Once the program is ready to be put into operation, the programmer prepares the written instructions for the people who will be operating and consulting the graphics program in their daily work.

Many diverse industries use computer graphics. In medicine, for example, physicians, nurses, and technicians can use computer graphics to view the internal organs of patients; scanners feed vital information about a patient's body to a computer, which interprets the input and displays a graphic representation of the patient's internal conditions. Computer graphics are used in flight simulators by airlines and NASA to train pilots and astronauts. Weather forecasters use computer graphics to show changes in weather patterns, and television newscasters use them to explain statistical information, such as stock market reports. Business people use computer-generated graphs and charts to make their reports more interesting and informative. Engineers use computer graphics to test the wear and stress of building materials and machine parts. The movie industry has found ingenious ways to use computer graphics for special effects. Professional artists have explored computer graphics for creating works of art.

Graphics programmers can be employed either by software manufacturing companies or by the companies that buy and use the software, known as end-users. The programmer who works for a software manufacturer will work on programs designed to fit the needs of prospective customers. For example, the programmer might work on a report-writing program for businesses and so develop simple ways for people to display and print statistical data in the form of diagrams, pie charts, and bar graphs. Programmers, working alone or as part of a team, must make the product user-friendly.

Computer graphics programmers who work for end-users have to tailor commercial software to fit their company's individual needs. If a company has limited computer needs or cannot afford to keep a programmer on payroll, it can call an independent consulting firm that has graphics programmers on staff and hire consultants for specific projects.

Requirements

High School

If you are interested in computer graphics programming take classes that satisfy the admission requirements of the college or university that you plan to attend. Most major universities have requirements for English, mathematics, science, and foreign languages. Other classes that are useful include physics, statistics, logic, computer science, and perhaps drafting. Since graphics programmers have to have an artistic sense of layout and design, art and photography courses can also be helpful.

Postsecondary Training

A bachelor's degree in computer science or a related field is essential for anyone wishing to enter the field of computer graphics programming. It is not a good idea, however, to major in graphics programming exclusively, unless you plan to go on to earn a master's degree or doctorate in the field. It is better for you to complete a general computer science curriculum, choosing electives such as graphics or business programming if they are available. In some universities that do not have computer science departments, computer graphics courses are available through the engineering department. Because there are many specialties within the field of computer graphics—such as art, mapmaking, animation, and computer-aided design (CAD)—you should examine the courses of study offered in several schools before choosing the one you wish to attend. An associate's degree or a certificate from a technical school may enable you to get a job as a keyboard operator or other paraprofessional with some firms, but future advancement is unlikely without additional education. Competition for all types of programming jobs is increasing and will limit the opportunities of those people with less than a bachelor's degree.

Exploring

If you are interested in a career in computer graphics programming, contact the computer science department of a local university. It may be possible to speak with a faculty member whose specialty is computer graphics or to sit in on a computer graphics class. Find out if there are any computer manufacturers or software firms in your area. By contacting their public relations departments, you might be able to speak with someone who works with or designs computer graphics systems or who can demonstrate how one works. You might also get involved with artistic projects at school, like theater set design and poster and banner design for extracurricular activities.

Employers

Graphics programmers are employed throughout the United States. Opportunities are best in large cities and suburbs where business and industry are active. Programmers who develop software systems work for software manufacturers, many of whom are in central California. There is also a concentration of software manufacturers in Boston, Chicago, and Atlanta. Programmers who adapt and tailor the software to meet specific needs of end-users work for those companies, many of which are scattered across the country.

Graphics programmers can also work in service centers that furnish computer time and software to businesses. Agencies, called job shops, employ programmers on short-term contracts. Self-employed graphics programmers can also work as consultants to small companies that cannot afford to employ full-time programmers.

Starting Out

Counselors and professors should be able to keep you informed of companies hiring computer programmers, including graphics programmers. Large manufacturing companies and computer software firms who employ many computer programmers send recruiters to universities with computer science departments. They usually work cooperatively with the guidance and placement departments. Guidance departments can also tell you about any firms

offering work-study programs and internships, which are excellent ways to gain training and experience in graphics programming. As employers become increasingly selective about new hires and seek to hold down the costs of in-house training, internships in computer programming are a great opportunity not only for on-the-job experience but also for a possible position after graduation from college.

Other possible sources of entry-level jobs are the numerous placement agencies that specialize in the field of computers. These agencies often advertise in major newspapers, technical journals, and computer magazines. They can also help match programmers to temporary jobs as more firms lower their personnel costs and hire freelance programmers to meet their needs. Programmers can also find out about new job opportunities by attending computer graphics conferences and networking with their professional peers. Some job openings are advertised in newspapers. There are many online career sites listed on the World Wide Web that post job openings, salary surveys, and current employment trends.

Advancement

The computer industry experiences high turnover, as large numbers of programmers and other employees move from company to company and from specialty to specialty. Some programmers leave their positions to accept higher-paying jobs with other firms, while others leave to start their own consulting companies. These extremely mobile conditions offer many opportunities both for job seekers and for those looking for career advancement.

In most companies, especially larger firms, advancement depends on an employee's experience and length of service. Beginning programmers might work alone on simple assignments after some initial instruction, or on a team with more experienced programmers. Either way, beginning programmers generally must work under close supervision. Because technology changes so rapidly, programmers must continuously update their training by taking courses sponsored by their employers or software vendors. For skilled workers who keep up-to-date with the latest technology, the prospects for advancement are good. In large organizations, they can be promoted to lead programmer and given supervisory responsibilities. Graphics programmers might be promoted to programmer-analysts, systems analysts, or to managerial positions. As employers increasingly contract out programming jobs, more opportunities should arise for experienced programmers with expertise in specific areas to work as consultants.

Because computer technology advances so rapidly, programmers who do not keep up with the field through additional college course work and attendance at seminars may find themselves blocked from advancement or even out of a job. Graphics programmers can benefit from membership in professional societies by attending conferences and seminars that these groups sponsor.

Earnings

Beginning graphics programmers earn between $35,000 and $45,000 per year. More experienced programmers or those with more education can earn between $50,000 and $57,000 per year. Programmers who work as independent consultants can earn more than $68,000 annually, but their salary may not be regular. Overall, those who work for private industry earn the most. Industry offers graphics programmers the highest earnings, as opportunities expand in aerospace, electronics, electrical machinery, and public utilities. Programmers who work as independent consultants or contractors can earn even more money, but their income is rarely constant or assured. Most of the best opportunities in this field are found in the Silicon Valley in Northern California or in Seattle, Washington, where Microsoft has its headquarters.

Those who work for corporations or computer firms usually receive full benefits, such as health insurance, paid vacation, and sick leave.

Work Environment

Most programmers work with state-of-the-art equipment. They usually put in 8 to 12 hours a day and work a 40- to 50-hour week. To meet deadlines or finish rush projects, they may work evenings and weekends. Programmers work alone or as part of a team and often consult with the end-users of the graphics program, as well as engineers and other specialists.

Programmers sometimes travel to attend seminars, conferences, and trade shows. Graphics programmers who work for software manufacturers may need to travel to assist current clients in their work or to solicit new customers for the software by demonstrating and discussing the product with potential buyers.

Graphics programmers in visual illustration departments of motion pictures or television production may spend months designing graphics for a clip that lasts minutes. There is often considerable pressure due to these deadlines.

Outlook

The demand for all types of computer programmers is strong, and employment is expected to grow much faster than the average for all occupations through 2006. This is especially true for graphics programmers, and the number of openings exceeds the number of qualified graphics programmers.

As more applications for computer graphics are explored in every field, the demand for graphics programmers will grow even more. One specialty expected to grow is computer-aided design/computer-aided manufacturing (CAD/CAM), which will need twice the number of programmers it now employs.

For More Information

Association for Computing Machinery
Special Interest Group on Computer Graphics (SIGGRAPH)
11 West 42nd Street
New York, NY 10036
Tel: 212-869-7440
Web: http://www.siggraph.org

Adobe Systems Inc.
345 Park Avenue
San Jose, CA 95110-2704
Tel: 408-536-6000
Web: http://www.adobe.com

Hardware Engineers

	School Subjects
Computer science Mathematics	
	Personal Skills
Mechanical/manipulative Technical/scientific	
	Work Environment
Primarily indoors Primarily one location	
	Minimum Education Level
Bachelor's degree	
	Salary Range
$35,705 to $43,312 to $100,000+	
	Certification or Licensing
Voluntary	
	Outlook
Much faster than the average	

Overview

Computer hardware engineers design, build, and test computer hardware—computer chips, circuit boards—as well as computer systems and software. They may also work with peripheral devices such as printers, scanners, modems, and monitors, among others. Hardware engineers are employed by a variety of companies, some of which specialize in business, accounting, science, or engineering. Most hardware engineers have a degree in computer science or engineering or equivalent computer background. According to the *Occupational Outlook Handbook,* there were about 212,000 computer engineers employed in the United States in the late 1990s.

History

What started as a specialty of electrical engineering has developed into a career field of its own. Today, many individuals interested in a career in one of the computer industry's most promising sectors turn to computer engineering. Computer engineers improve and repair computers and implement changes needed to keep up with the demand for faster and stronger computers and more complex software programs. Some specialize in the design of computer or peripheral parts—the hardware—such as memory chips, motherboards, or microprocessors. Others specialize in creating and organizing information systems for businesses and the government.

More and more businesses rely on computers for information networking, accessing the Internet, and data processing for their daily activities. Also, computers are now affordable, allowing many families to purchase systems. Peripherals, such as printers, scanners, and disk drives, are popular accessories available to complete a variety of tasks. The Institute of Electrical and Electronic Engineers (IEEE) predicts that much of the industry's growth will be directed toward the private sector. Computer engineers are needed to develop and improve technology for consumer products, such as cellular phones, microwave ovens, compact disc players, high-televisions, and video games. Engineers turn to program tools, such as computer-aided design (CAD), to help them create new products. CAD programs are often used with computer-aided manufacturing (CAM) programs to produce three-dimensional drawings that can easily be altered or manipulated, and direct the actual production of hardware components.

The Job

Calvin Prior is a network systems administrator for TASC, a nonprofit social service agency headquartered in Chicago, Illinois. He is responsible for the day-to-day operations of a state-wide network of 300+ servers. Calvin starts work early; most mornings he's at his desk by 7:30 AM. His first task of the day is making sure the network files from the previous day backed up successfully. Then he checks for email and voice mail messages and promptly responds to urgent problems.

Daily meetings are held to keep informed on department business. "It's very short and informal," says Calvin. "We discuss urgent business or upcoming projects and schedules." The rest of the morning is spent working on various projects, troubleshooting systems, or phone work with TASC's remote offices. After a quick lunch break, and if no network breakdowns or glitches occur, Calvin usually spends his afternoons researching hardware products or responding to user requests.

The workload changes daily, leaving some days more hectic than others. "It's important to be flexible," says Calvin. "And be good at multi-tasking." If a major problem cannot be solved over the phone, Calvin must travel to the source. Solutions are not always simple; some require changing hardware or redesigning the system. Calvin often upgrades or reworks systems in the early morning, late at night, or on weekends to minimize the disruption of work. Major network problems require a complete shutdown of the entire system. "The less number of servers on the network, the better," he says.

Engineering professionals like Calvin must be familiar with different network systems, such as Local Area Networks (LAN) and Wide Area Networks (WAN), as well as programming languages suited to their companies' needs. Many work as part of a team of specialists who use elements of science, math, and electronics to improve existing technology or implement solutions.

Requirements

High School

Calvin credits high school computer and electronics classes and programming courses as giving him a head start in this career. You should also take speech and writing courses so that you will be able to communicate effectively with co-workers and clients.

Postsecondary Training

Calvin initially studied electrical engineering at the University of Illinois, Champaign-Urbana, but transferred and eventually graduated with an associate's degree in electronics from Parkland Community College. The hands-on approach at Parkland appealed to Calvin. "Most of our classes were held in the late afternoon and evening because many of the instructors held real computer industry jobs in addition to their teaching duties."

Certification or Licensing

Not all computer professionals are certified—the deciding factor seems to be whether certification is required by their employers Many companies offer tuition reimbursement, or incentives, to those who earn certification. Certification is available in a variety of specialties. The Institute for

Certification of Computing Professionals (ICCP), for example, offers the designation Certified Computing Professional, after successful completion of required study and examination. Certification is held by many as a measure of industry knowledge as well as leverage when negotiating salary.

Other Requirements

What do companies look for in new hires? Industry insiders say patience, self-motivation, and a broad range of computer skills. Flexibility is another important skill. Often, a number of projects are worked on simultaneously, so according to Calvin, "multi-tasking is important."

Employers

Computer hardware engineers are employed in nearly every industry by small and large corporations alike. According to the *OOH,* the majority of hardware engineers are employed by the computer and data processing and electronics manufacturing industries.

Jobs are plentiful nationwide, though salary averages, as reported by a recent *Computerworld* survey, tend to be higher in New York City and Los Angeles. Note, however, that these cities are notorious for their high costof living, which, in the end, may offset a higher income.

Starting Out

Education and solid work experience will open industry doors. Though a bachelor's degree is a minimum requirement for most corporate giants, some companies, smaller ones especially, will hire based largely on work experience and practical training. Many computer professionals employed in the computer industry for some time do not have traditional electrical engineering or computer science degrees, but rather moved up on the basis of their work record. However, if you aspire to a management position, or want to work as a teacher, then having a college degree is a necessity.

Large computer companies aggressively recruit on campus armed with signing bonuses and other incentives. Employment opportunities are posted in newspaper want ads daily, with some papers devoting a separate section to computer-related positions. The Internet offers a wealth of employment information plus several sites for browsing job openings or to post your resume. Most companies maintain a Web page where they post employment opportunities or solicit resumes.

Like other fields in the computer industry, demand for computer engineers is so great, schools can't seem to supply enough graduates. Calvin agrees. "There is a lack of quality workers," he says. "One of our biggest problems is being understaffed."

Advancement

Many companies hire new grads to work as junior engineers. Problem-solving skills and the ability to implement solutions are important to this entry-level job. With enough work experience, junior engineers can move into positions that focus on a particular area in the computer industry, say networks or peripherals. Landing a senior-level engineering position, systems architect for example, is possible after considerable work experience and study. You should hone your computer skills to the highest level—that means keeping abreast of the latest technology with continuing education, certification, or even advanced computer study. Many high-level engineers hold a master's degree or better.

Some computer professionals working on the technical side of the industry opt to switch over to the marketing side of the business. Advancement opportunities here may include positions in product management or sales.

Earnings

According to a 1998 National Association of Colleges and Employers salary survey, hardware design and development engineers with a bachelor's degree in computer science earn an average starting salary of $43,312. In comparison, graduates with an engineering background earn an average annual salary between $35,705 and $40,750. Graduates of master's programs in computer engineering have average starting salaries of about $50,650; starting salaries for holders of doctorates are even higher.

The demand for talented and educated workers is very strong, causing many companies to offer incentives or signing bonuses to lure prospective employees. Other job perks, besides the usual benefit package—insurance, vacation, sick time, profit sharing—may include stock options, continuing education or training, tuition reimbursement, flexible hours, and child care or other on-site services.

Work Environment

Most hardware engineers work 40- to 50-hour weeks or more depending on the project to which they are assigned. Weekend work is common with some positions. Contrary to popular perceptions, hardware engineers do not spend their workdays cooped up in their offices. Instead, they spend the majority of their time meeting, planning, and working with various staff members from different levels of management and technical expertise. Since it takes numerous workers to take a project from start to finish, team players are in high demand.

Outlook

Computer engineering will be one of the three fastest growing occupations through the year 2006, according to the *Occupational Outlook Handbook*. Industry growth can be attributed to factors such as greater business use of the Internet; the networking of information and resources within a company; and technical advancements. Investment in a college education—good major choices are engineering, Management Information Systems (MIS), computer science, or solid computer-related courses, such as computer systems analysis, computer programming, among others, will help you secure a promising employment future. Also, don't forget the value of on-the-job training and work experience with networks, databases, and other systems.

In addition to new job opportunities, many positions will open as a result of current computer professionals leaving the industry due to retirement or other reasons.

For More Information

For information regarding the computer industry, career opportunities as a computer engineer, or the association's membership requirements, contact:

Association for Computing Machinery
1515 Broadway, 17th Floor
New York, NY 10036-5701
Tel: 212-869-7440
Email: SIGS@acm.org
Web: http://www.acm.org

For certification information, contact:

Institute for Certification of Computing Professionals
2200 East Devon Avenue, Suite 247
Des Plaines, IL 60018-4503
Tel: 847-299-4227
Web: http://www.iccp.org

For information on a career in computer engineering, computer scholarships, or a copy of Computer Magazine, contact:

The Computer Society
1730 Massachusetts Avenue, NW
Washington, DC 20036-1992
Tel: 202-371-0101
Web: http://www.computer.org

For employment information, links to online career sites for computer professionals, and background on the industry, contact:

Institute of Electrical and Electronics Engineers (IEEE)
3 Park Avenue, 17th Floor
New York, NY 10016-5997
Tel: 212-419-7900
Web: http://www.ieee.org

For a history of computers, a description of careers in computer engineering, educational resources, or computer-related interactive exhibits, contact:

The Computer Museum
Web: http://www.tcm.org

Internet Content Developers

	School Subjects
Computer science Mathematics	

	Personal Skills
Communication/ideas Technical/scientific	

	Work Environment
Primarily indoors Primarily one location	

	Minimum Education Level
Bachelor's degree	

	Salary Range
$30,000 to $50,000 to $74,000	

	Certification or Licensing
Recommended	

	Outlook
Much faster than the average	

Overview

An *Internet content developer,* otherwise known as a *Web developer* or *Web designer,* is responsible for the creation of an Internet site. Most of the time, this is a public Web site, but it can also be a private network using Internet technology. Web developers are employed by a wide range of employers from small entrepreneurial and large corporate businesses to Internet consulting firms.

History

With the explosive growth of the Internet, companies have flocked to use Internet technology to communicate worldwide—with employees, customers, clients, buyers, future stockholders, and so on. As a result, these companies need people who can create sites to fit their needs and the needs of their target audiences.

In the early years of the Internet, most information presented was text only with no pictures. Today, a few sites still use a text-only format, but the vast majority have evolved to use the latest technologies—graphics, video, audio, and interactive forms and applications.

For most companies, the first Internet sites were created and maintained by a sole individual who was a jack-of-all-trades. Today, these sites are often designed, implemented, and managed by entire departments composed of numerous individuals who specialize in specific areas of Web site work. The Web developer is the one with the technical knowledge of programming to implement the ideas and goals of the organization into a smoothly flowing, informative, interesting Web site. Because of evolving technology, the future will require more specialized and complex skills and technological expertise of Web developers.

The Job

After determining the overall goals, layout, and performance limitations of the Web site (most likely the job of the Webmaster (see the article "Webmasters"), with input from marketing, sales, advertising, and other departments), an Internet or Web content developer designs the site and writes the code necessary to run and navigate it. To make the site, working knowledge of the latest Internet programming languages, such as Perl, Visual Basic, CGI, Java, ActiveX, C++, and HTML, is a must. The developer must also be up-to-date on the latest in graphic file formats and other Web production tools.

The concept of the site must be translated to a general layout. The layout must be turned into a set of pages, which are designed, written, and edited. Those pages are then converted into the proper code so that they can be placed on the server. Software packages exist to help the developer create the sites. However, software packages often use templates to create sites that have the same general look to them—not a good thing if the site is to stand out and look original. Also, no one software package does it all, and additional scripts or special features—banners with the latest advertising slogan, spinning logos, forms that provide data input from users, and easy online ordering—are often needed to add punch to a site.

Perhaps the trickiest part of the job is effectively integrating the needs of the organization with the needs of the customer. For example, the organization might want the content to be visually cutting edge and entertaining, however, the targeted customer might not have the modem speed needed to view those highly graphical pages and might prefer to get "just the facts" quickly. The developer must find a happy medium and deliver the information in a practical yet interesting manner.

Requirements

High School

In high school, take as many courses as possible in computer science, science, and mathematics. These classes will provide you with a good foundation in computer basics and analytical-thinking skills. You should also take English and speech classes in order to hone your written and verbal communication skills.

Postsecondary Training

Web developers typically hold bachelor's degrees in computer science or computer programming—although some have degrees in noncomputer areas, such as marketing, graphic design, or information systems. Regardless of educational background, you need to have an understanding of computers and computer networks and a knowledge of Internet programming languages. Formal college training in these languages may be hard to come by because of the rapid evolution of the Internet. What's hot today might be obsolete tomorrow. Because of this volatility, most of the postsecondary training comes from hands-on experience. This is best achieved through internships or entry-level positions. One year of experience working on a site is invaluable toward landing a job in the field.

Certification or Licensing

Because there is no central governing organization or association for this field, certification is not required. Certifications are available, however, from various vendors of development software applications and are helpful in proving your abilities to an employer. The more certifications you have, the more you have to offer.

Other Requirements

A good Internet content developer balances technological know-how with creativity. You must be able to make a site stand out from the sea of other sites on the Web. For example, if your company is selling a product on the Web, your site needs to "scream" the unique qualities and benefits of the product.

Working with Internet technologies, you must be able to adapt quickly to change. It is not uncommon to learn a new programming language, get comfortable using it, and then have to learn another new language, scrapping the old one. If you're a quick study, then you should have an advantage.

Exploring

Does the career of Internet content developer sound interesting? If so, there are many ways to learn more about the field. You can read national news magazines, newspapers, and trade magazines or surf the Web for information about Internet careers. You can also visit a variety of Web sites to study what makes them appealing or not so appealing. Does your high school have a Web site? If so, get involved in the planning and creation of new content for it. If not, talk to your computer teachers about creating one, or create your own site at home.

Employers

Everyone is getting online these days, from the Fortune 500 companies to the smallest of mom-and-pop shops. The smaller companies might have one person in charge of everything Web-related: the server, the site, the security, and so on. The larger companies employ departments of many, each one taking on specific responsibilities.

Obvious places of employment are Internet consulting firms. Some firms specialize in Web development, or Web site management; other firms offer services relating to all aspects of Web site design, creation, management, and maintenance.

The Internet is worldwide; thus, Internet jobs are available worldwide. Wherever there is a business connected to the Internet, you can find a job related to the Internet.

Starting Out

If you are looking for a job as a Web developer, remember that experience is key. College courses are important, but if you graduate and have lots of book knowledge and no experience, you're going to get a slow start. If at all possible, get internships while in school and get as many as you can.

Use the Internet to find a job on the Internet. Use the various search engines and search for the words "Web Jobs." Check out some of the online trade magazines for a job bank or classified section.

Advancement

If you get a job as a Web developer, the next step up the career ladder might be to move to a larger company where the Web site presence consists of more pages (perhaps as many as 1,000) and more complex. Another option is to become a *Webmaster*. Webmasters generally have the responsibility of overseeing all aspects (technical, management, maintenance, marketing, and organization) of a Web site.

Earnings

An entry-level position in Web development at a small company pays around $30,000. As you gain experience or move to a larger company, you might make $50,000. The top of the pay scale hits around $74,000. Benefits include paid vacation, paid holidays, paid sick days, health insurance, dental insurance, life insurance, personal days, and bonuses.

Differences in pay tend to follow the differences found in other careers: the Northeast pays more than the Midwest or South, and men are paid more than women (although this may change as the number of women rivals the number of men employed in these jobs).

Work Environment

Work is done at the computer, which requires a climate-controlled environment. Thus, you are primarily indoors, at a desk, working on a computer. Most of your work is done alone, however developers consult frequently with the Webmaster and others who work with them to write or edit the content of a site.

Outlook

The field of Internet content developer, like the Internet itself, is growing much faster than the average. As more and more companies look to go worldwide, they need employees who have the ability and expertise to create the sites to bring their products, services, and corporate images to the Net. Web developers can expect Internet technology to continue to evolve and change at a rapid pace.

For More Information

The Association of Internet Professionals represents the worldwide community of people employed in Internet-related fields.

Association of Internet Professionals (AIP)
9200 Sunset Boulevard, Suite 710
Los Angeles, CA 90069
Tel: 800-JOIN-AIP
Web: http://www.association.org/index.html

Internet Security Specialists

Overview

An *Internet security specialist* is someone who is responsible for protecting a company's network, which can be accessed through the Internet, from intrusion by outsiders. These intruders are referred to as *hackers* (or *crackers*), and the process of breaking into a system is called *hacking* (or *cracking*). Internet security often falls under the jurisdiction of computer systems engineering and network administration within a company. Any company that has an Internet presence might employ an Internet security specialist. This includes all kinds of companies of all sizes anywhere around the world. Some Internet security specialists work for consulting firms that specialize in Internet security. Internet security specialists are sometimes known as *Internet security administrators, Internet security engineers, information security technicians, and network security consultants.*

History

Hacking first began in the telecommunications industry. Cracking a telephone system was called *phreaking*. It involved learning how the telephone system worked and then manipulating it. As PCs began to hook up to networks via telephone lines and modems, phreaking took on new meaning and the information at risk took on greater importance.

November 2, 1988, is sometimes called Black Thursday by pioneers of the Internet community. On that day, a single program, later called a worm, was released onto the early form of the Internet (then called the ARPANET) and quickly rendered thousands of connected computers useless. The creator of the program, Robert Morris, Jr., shocked at how quickly it was spreading, sent an anonymous message to Internet users telling how to kill the worm and prevent it from infecting more computers. Morris was convicted of a federal felony and sentenced to three years probation, 400 hours of community service, and $10,050 in fines.

With the release of the Morris Worm, a group of computer experts from the National Computer Security Center, part of the National Security Agency, gathered to discuss the susceptibility to attack of Internet-connected computers. Out of these meetings, the Computer Emergency Response Team (CERT) Coordination Center, a federally funded organization that monitors and reports activity on the Internet, was started at Carnegie Mellon University. This is considered the beginning of Internet security.

The Job

The duties of an Internet security specialist vary depending on where he or she works, how big the company is, and the degree of sensitivity of the information that is being protected. The duties are also affected by whether the specialist is a consultant or works in-house.

Internet security usually falls under the jurisdiction of a Systems Engineering or Systems Administration department. A large company that deals with sensitive information probably has one or two Internet security specialists who devote all of their time and energy to Internet security. Many firms, upon connecting to the Internet, give security duties to the person who is in charge of systems administration. A smaller firm might hire an *Internet security consultant* to come in and set up security systems and software.

A *firewall* is a system set up to act as a barrier of protection between the outside world of the Internet and the company. You can tell the firewall to limit access or permit access to users. The Internet security specialist configures it to define the kind of access to allow or restrict.

Primarily, Internet security specialists are in charge of monitoring the flow of information through the firewall. Security specialists must be able to write code and configure the software to alert them when certain kinds of activities occur. They can tell the program what activity to allow and what to disallow. They can even program the software to page them or send them an email if some questionable activity occurs. Logs are kept of all access to the network. Security specialists monitor the logs and watch for anything out of the ordinary. If they see something strange, they must make a judgment call as to whether the activity was innocent or malicious. Then they must investigate and do some detective work—perhaps even tracking down the user who initiated the action. In other instances, they might have to create a new program to prevent that action from happening again.

Sometimes the Internet security specialist is in charge of virus protection or encryption and user authentication systems. *Viruses* are programs written with the express purpose of harming a hard drive and can enter a network through email attachments or infected floppy disks. Encryption and authentication are used with any network activity that requires transmission of delicate information, such as passwords, user accounts, or even credit card numbers.

Secondary duties can include security administrative work, such as establishing security policies for the company, or security engineering duties, which are more technical in nature. For example, some companies might deal with such sensitive information that the company forbids any of its information to be transmitted over email. Programs can be written to disallow transmission of any company product information or to alert the specialist when this sensitive information is transmitted. The security specialist also might be in charge of educating employees on security policies concerning their network.

Internet security consultants have a different set of duties. Consultants are primarily in charge of designing and implementing solutions to their clients' security problems. They must be able to listen to and detect the needs of the client and then meet their needs. They perform routine assessments to determine if there are insecurities within the clients' network and, if there are, find ways to correct them. A company might employ a consultant as a preventive measure to avoid attacks. Other times, a consultant might be called on after a security breach has been detected to find the problem, fix it, and even track down the perpetrator.

Secondary duties of an Internet security consultant include management and administrative duties. He or she manages various accounts and must be able to track them and maintain paperwork and communications. Senior consultants have consultants who report to them and take on supervisory responsibilities in addition to their primary duties.

A benefit of using consultants is bringing new perspective to an old problem. Often times, they can use their many experiences with other clients to help find solutions. The consultant does not work solely with one client but has multiple accounts. He or she spends a lot of time traveling and must be reachable at a moment's notice.

Requirements

High School

If you are a high school student and think you want to get into the Internet security industry, first and foremost you need to get involved in computer science/programming classes. Don't just book learn, however. Hands-on experience is key and probably is what will get you your first job. Spend time in the school computer lab, learn how computers work, dabble with the latest technologies. Most of those employed in the field today began at a young age just playing around. What began as their hobby eventually turned into an enjoyable and challenging career.

If you plan on getting into management or consulting, a well-rounded background in communications is important. Get involved in local clubs or perhaps student government.

Postsecondary Training

College courses are valuable for showing employers that you have what it takes to learn. However, most colleges do not have specific programs in Internet security. Most offer computer science, networking, and programming-related degrees, which are highly recommended. Computer lab courses teach how to work with a team to solve problems and complete assignments—something that you will probably do in this field—especially in the consulting business. Programming requires an understanding of mathematics and algorithms. Law enforcement classes are also beneficial. By learning the mindset of the criminal, you can better protect your client or employer. Last, being versed in intellectual property laws is important because you will be working with transmitting and protecting sensitive information as it travels to various locations.

Internships are the best way to gain hands-on experience. They offer real-life situations and protected work environments where you can see what Internet security is all about. Internships are not common, however—mostly because of security problems that arise from bringing inexperienced young people into contact with sensitive, confidential information. The majority of exposed hackers are under 20 years of age so it is easy to understand companies' unwillingness to offer internships.

On-the-job training is the best way to break into Internet security. Without experience, you can never land a job in the field.

Certification or Licensing

There is no central professional association or organization that grants certification for Internet security specialists. Certification is available from various vendors of Internet security software and other products. Each vendor offers its own training and certification program, which varies from company to company. Some certifications can be completed in a matter of a few days; others take years. The majority of those employed in the field are not certified; however, certification is a trend and is considered an advantage. The more certifications you have, the more you have to offer a company.

The Internet is constantly evolving, and Internet technology changes so rapidly that it is vital for the Internet security specialist to stay on top of current technology. After all, if a hacker has knowledge of cutting edge technology and can use it to break into a system, the security specialist must be trained to counter those attacks. Security specialists must be well versed in the same cutting edge technology. Often, the vendor creating the most current technology is the best training source. In the future, the technology is likely to become more complex, and so is the training. Ideally, product certification coupled with a few years of hands-on experience qualifies you for advancement.

Other Requirements

If you like doing the same thing on a daily basis (like monitoring network activity logs and writing code), a job as Internet security specialist might be good for you. On the other hand, you must be flexible so that you are ready to meet each new challenge with fresh ideas. Some hackers are creative, and it is important that the security specialist be just as creative.

Consultants must be well organized because they work with many accounts at once. Communication skills are important because consultants often deal with management and try to sell them on the importance of security software. They must also be willing to travel on a regular basis to visit their accounts.

Exploring

If you think Internet security is a field you might want to get into, play around on your computer. Find out how it works. Check out programming books from the local library and learn how to write simple code.

High school science clubs and competitions are a great way to try your hand at computer programming. They are great places to design and implement systems and solutions in a nonthreatening atmosphere. You can also work with other students to get accustomed to working in teams.

The most obvious place to learn about the Internet is on the Internet. Surf the Web and research the many security issues facing users today. Check out the various information security Web sites and organizations that deal with Internet security. Use a search engine and the keywords "Internet AND Security" or "Network AND Security" or "Information AND Security." This search will also bring up sites of consulting firms where you can get an idea of the services these firms offer.

National news magazines, newspapers, and trade magazines are great sources of information. You can find out a lot about current trends and hiring practices there. Look up the classified section and get an idea of what kind of market it is and where the jobs are.

Employers

Any company with an Internet presence (Web site, FTP site, email service, etc.) has the potential for security breaches and can benefit from the work and advice of an Internet Security Specialist. Depending on the size of the company and the nature of the company's business, it might use outside consultants or employ one part-time or several full-time employees.

An obvious place of employment is an Internet security consulting firm. These Internet security consulting firms are cropping up all over the country. In fact, some business consulting firms like Ernst & Young are adding Internet security branches to their current businesses.

Data forensics is another growing business where Internet security specialists are hired to act as detectives to find culprits who break into computer networks. The Federal Bureau of Investigation has recently set up Computer Crime Squads in seven cities in the United States.

Starting Out

It is unlikely that someone fresh out of high school or college will get a job as an Internet security specialist. Although education is important, experience is key in the field. Certifications are great, but again, they do not mean much without experience. If you can, get an internship in systems administration or engineering and you might happen upon an experience or two with the security aspect of that company. Above all, work hard, get some good references, and keep yourself clean. It is not uncommon for those applying for security positions to have background checks or at least have their list of references closely interviewed to make sure the applicants are trustworthy individuals. In fact, many companies prefer to hire individuals who have been recommended to them directly by someone they know and trust.

Many who are in Internet security began in PC technical support and moved to systems administration or engineering. These jobs often include security responsibilities which then lead to positions focusing primarily on security.

If word-of-mouth doesn't get you a job, check the classifieds—both in the local newspapers and trade magazines. And don't forget the World Wide Web. Many places post job openings on their Web sites.

Advancement

If you start out as an Internet security specialist, the next step might be to move up to senior Internet security specialist at the same company. Or, if the company where you work is small, you might move to the same position at a larger company or at a company whose data is more sensitive.

Likewise, as an Internet security consultant, you can advance to senior Internet security consultant. And if you are the best and the brightest, you can become a *sneaker* or part of a *tiger team*. A sneaker and a tiger team are the best in the field who are called in to crack a system on purpose in order to find security holes and then patch them.

Earnings

The field of Internet security is a lucrative business and the salary potential is growing. The low end of the pay scale is $25,000 a year and is probably what you would make in an entry-level position at a small company. The majority of Internet security specialists make between $50,000 and $75,000 a year. If you have a lot of experience and an excellent reputation in the industry, you can pull in as much as $120,000 a year.

Salaries increase with the size of the company and the nature of the information you are charged with protecting. Extremely confidential information in an industry such as the automotive industry would bring much greater pay than working at a small family business.

If you live in the Northeast, you can expect to be paid more than if you live in the Midwest. Men generally make more than women. The highest paying industries are manufacturing, computers, and communication/utilities companies. Military and government sectors pay the least.

Benefits include paid vacation, paid sick days, personal days, medical and dental insurance, and bonuses.

Work Environment

Because Internet security specialists work with computers and computers require a controlled atmosphere, the work environment is typically indoors in a well lit, climate-controlled office. There is no hard labor, but you can expect many hours of sitting in front of a computer screen using a keyboard. Work is generally done alone—although a consultant might train an in-house person on how to use certain software.

Most work schedules require 40 to 50 hours a week. Consultants travel frequently, and their work schedules do not necessarily follow typical nine-to-five working hours. There are instances where additional hours are required—for example, if a serious breach of security is detected and time is of the essence to fix it. It is not uncommon for employees to be on call so they can respond quickly to critical situations.

Although you might expect this line of work to be stressful, it generally is not. Most businesses see the value of protecting their information and budget appropriately for the necessary tools, equipment, and staff.

Outlook

The outlook for Internet security is that it will grow much faster than the average. The number of companies with a presence on the Internet is exploding. As these companies connect their private networks to the public Internet, they will need to protect their confidential information. Currently, the demand for Internet security specialists is greater than the supply, and this trend is expected to continue as the number of businesses connecting to the Internet continues to grow.

Until now, most Internet security specialists have gotten by with general skills. In the future, however, they will need to become more specialized. Staying on top of the most current technologies will be one of the biggest challenges.

Because of the ever-changing new technology, educational institutions will continue to have difficulty in training students for this field. Vendors and on-the-job experience will continue to provide the best training.

For More Information

A federally funded organization, the CERT Coordination Center studies, monitors, and publishes security-related activity and research. It also provides an incident response service to those who have been cracked.

CERT Coordination Center
Software Engineering Institute, Carnegie Mellon University
Pittsburgh, PA 15213-3890
Tel: 412-268-7090
Email: cert@cert.org
Web: http://www.cert.org/

A professional organization for information security professionals, CSI provides education and training for its members.

Computer Security Institute
600 Harrison Street
San Francisco, CA 94107
Tel: 415-905-2626
Web: http://www.gocsi.com/

In addition to providing security products and services, ICSA has a professional membership organization and also runs consortia groups that share research and information on current security issues.

International Computer Security Association (ICSA)
Corporate Headquarters
12379-C Sunrise Valley Drive
Reston, VA 20191-3422
Tel: 703-453-0500
Email: info@icsa.net
Web: http://www.icsa.net/

Information Security Magazine is published by ICSA and is a trade magazine for the information security professional.

Information Security Magazine
106 Access Road
Norwood, MA 02062
Tel: 781-255-0200
Web: http://www.infosecuritymag.com/

Quality Assurance Testers

	School Subjects
Computer science Mathematics	

	Personal Skills
Mechanical/manipulative Technical/scientific	

	Work Environment
Primarily indoors Primarily one location	

	Minimum Education Level
High school diploma	

	Salary Range
$25,000 to $49,000 to $60,000+	

	Certification or Licensing
None available	

	Outlook
Faster than the average	

Overview

Quality assurance testers examine new or modified computer software applications to evaluate whether or not they perform at the desired level. Testers might also verify that computer-automated quality assurance programs function properly. Their work entails trying to crash computer programs by punching in certain characters very quickly, for example, or by clicking the mouse on the border of an icon. They keep very close track of the combinations they enter so that they can replicate the situation if the program does crash. They also offer opinions on the user-friendliness of the program. Any problems they find or suggestions they have are reported in detail both verbally and in writing to supervisors.

History

The first major advances in modern computer technology were made during World War II. After the war, it was thought that the enormous size of computers, which easily took up the space of entire warehouses, would limit their use to huge government projects. Accordingly, the 1950 census was computer processed.

The introduction of semiconductors to computer technology made possible smaller and less expensive computers. Businesses began adapting computers to their operations as early as 1954. Within 30 years, computers had revolutionized the way people work, play, and shop. Today, computers are everywhere, from businesses of all kinds, to government agencies, charitable organizations, and private homes. Over the years, the technology has continued to shrink computer size and increase speed at an unprecedented rate.

Engineers have been able to significantly increase the memory capacity and processing speed of computer hardware. These technological advances enable computers to work effectively processing more information than ever before. Consequently, more sophisticated software applications have been created. These programs offer extremely user-friendly and sophisticated working environments that would not have been possible on older, slower computers. In addition, the introduction of CD-ROMs to the mass computer market enabled the production of complex programs stored on compact disks.

As software applications became more complicated, the probability and sheer number of errors increased. Quality assurance departments were expanded to develop methods for testing software applications for errors, or "bugs." Quality assurance is now a branch of science and engineering in its own right. "Testing is finally being recognized as an important phase of the product cycle," says Steve Devinney, vice president and managing director of the Quality Assurance Institute in Orlando, Florida. The importance of good testing procedures came to the forefront of the computer industry in the late 1990s with the emergence of the Year 2000 (Y2K) problems. "Testers were second-class citizens," says Steve. "The thought was that if the project was running late, you could just skip the testing. Now, because of the Y2K situation, testing is becoming more important."

The field has changed with the advent of automated testing tools. As technology continues to advance, many quality assurance tests are automated. Quality assurance testers also "test the tests," that is, look for errors in the programs that test the software. There will always be a need for quality assurance testers, however, since they, not another computer, are best suited to judge a program from a user's point of view. "The use of tools will increase, but they can never replace humans," notes Steve.

The Job

Before manufacturers can introduce a product on the consumer market, they must run extensive tests on its safety and quality. Failing to do so thoroughly can be very expensive, resulting in liability lawsuits when unsafe products harm people or in poor sales when products do not perform well. The nature and scope of quality assurance testing varies greatly. High-tech products, such as computers and other electronics, require extremely detailed technical testing.

Computer software applications undergo a specific series of tests designed to anticipate and help solve problems that users might encounter. Quality assurance testers examine new or modified computer software applications to evaluate whether they function at the desired level. They also verify that computer automated quality assurance programs perform in accordance with designer specifications and user requirements. This includes checking the product's functionality (how it will work), network performance (how it will work with other products), installation (how to put it in), and configuration (how it is set up).

Some quality assurance testers spend most of their time working on software programs or playing computer games, just as an average consumer might. If it is a game, for example, they play it over and over again for hours, trying to make moves quickly or slowly to "crash" it. A program crashes if it completely stops functioning due to, among other things, an inability to process incoming commands. For other types of programs, like word processors, quality assurance testers might type very quickly or click the mouse on inappropriate areas of the screen to see if the program can correctly handle such usage.

Quality assurance testers keep detailed records of the hours logged working on individual programs. They write reports based on their observations about how well the program performed in different situations, always imagining how typical, nontechnical users would judge it. The goal is to make the programs more efficient, user-friendly, fun, and visually exciting. Lastly, they keep track of the precise combinations of keystrokes and mouse clicks that made the program crash. This type of record is very important because it enables supervisors and programmers to replicate the problem. Then they can better isolate its source and begin to design a solution.

Programs to be tested arrive in the quality assurance department after programmers and software engineers have finished the initial version. Each program is assigned a specific number of tests, and the quality assurance testers go to work. They make sure that the correct tests are run, write reports, and send the program back to the programmers for revisions and correction. Some testers have direct contact with the programmers. After evaluating a product, they might meet with programmers to describe the problems they encountered and suggest ways for solving glitches. Others report solely to a quality assurance supervisor.

When automated tests are to be run, quality assurance testers tell the computer which tests to administer and then make sure they run smoothly by watching a computer screen for interruption codes and breakdown signals. They also interpret test results, verifying their credibility by running them through special programs that check for accuracy and reliability. Then, they write reports explaining their conclusions.

Some quality assurance testers have direct contact with users experiencing problems with their software. They listen closely to customer complaints to determine the precise order of keystrokes that led to the problem. Then, they attempt to duplicate the problem on their own computers and run in-depth tests to figure out the cause. Eventually, if the problem is not simply a result of user error, they inform programmers and software engineers of the problems and suggest certain paths to take in resolving them.

Some quality assurance testers with solid work experience and bachelor's degrees in a computer-related field might go on to work as *quality assurance analysts*. Analysts write and revise the quality standards for each software program that passes through the department. They also use computer programming skills to create the tests and programs the quality assurance testers use to test the programs. They might evaluate proposals for new software applications, advising management about whether the program will be able to achieve its goals. Since they know many software applications inside and out, they might also train users on how to work with various programs.

Requirements

High School

Interested in becoming a quality assurance tester? If so, then take as many computer classes as possible to become familiar with how to effectively operate computer software and hardware. Math and science courses are very helpful for teaching the necessary analytical skills. English and speech classes will help you improve your verbal and written communication skills, which are also essential to the success of quality assurance testers.

Postsecondary Training

It is debatable whether a bachelor's degree is necessary to become a quality assurance tester. Some companies require a bachelor's degree in computer science, while others prefer people who come from the business sector who have a small amount of computer experience because they best match the technical level of the software's typical users. If testers are interested in advancement, however, a bachelor's degree is almost a mandate.

Most companies offer in-house training on how to test their particular products, since few universities or colleges offer courses on quality assurance testing. "Because no 'state-of-the-art' exists for software testing, especially in packaged software, many companies must scrape together their own ideas of testing competence, or hire outside consultants who can provide useful training," writes James Bach in *The Challenge of Training Testers*.

Certification or Licensing

As the Information Technology industry becomes more competitive, the necessity for management to be able to distinguish professional and skilled individuals in the field becomes mandatory, according to the Quality Assurance Institute. Certification demonstrates a level of understanding in carrying out relevant principles and practices, as well as providing a common ground for communication among professionals in the field of software quality. The organization offers certification programs in certified quality analyst, certified software test engineer, and certified assessor.

Other Requirements

Quality assurance testers need superior verbal and written communication skills, according to information supplied by ST Labs/Data Dimensions, Inc. They also must show a proficiency in critical and analytical thinking and be able to critique something diplomatically. Quality assurance testers should have an eye for detail, be focused, and have a lot of enthusiasm because sometimes the work is monotonous and repetitive, notes ST Labs/Data Dimensions, Inc. Testers should definitely enjoy the challenge of breaking the system.

Some companies recommend testers have some programming skills in languages such as C, C++, SQL, or Visual Basic. Others prefer testers with no programming ability. "The most important thing is that testers understand the business and the testing tools with which they are working," says Steve.

"You have to be a good problem solver and detective. Testing is a difficult job."

Exploring

Students interested in quality assurance and other computer jobs should gain wide exposure to computer systems and programs of all kinds. ST Labs/Data Dimensions, Inc. offers the following advice. Become a power user. Get a computer at home, borrow a friend's, or check out the computer lab at your school. Work on becoming comfortable using the Windows programs and thoroughly learn how to operate all of the computer, including the hardware. Look for bugs in your software at home and practice writing them up. Keep up with emerging technologies. If you cannot get hands-on experience with new technologies, read about them. Join a computer group or society. Read books on testing and familiarize yourself with methodology, terminology, the development cycle, and where testing fits in. Subscribe to newsletters or magazines that are related to testing or quality assurance. Get involved with online newsgroups that deal with the subject. Check out sites on the World Wide Web that deal with quality assurance.

If you live in an area where numerous computer software companies are located, like the Silicon Valley in northern California, for example, you might be able to secure a part-time or summer job as a quality assurance tester. In addition, investigate the possibility of spending an afternoon with an employed quality assurance tester to find out what a typical day is like.

Employers

Quality assurance testers are employed throughout the United States. Opportunities are best in large cities and suburbs where business and industry are active. Many testers work for software manufacturers, a cluster of which are located in Silicon Valley, in nothern California. There are also concentrations of software manufacturers in Boston, Chicago, and Atlanta.

Starting Out

Positions in the field of quality assurance can be obtained several different ways. Many universities and colleges host computer job fairs on campus throughout the year that include representatives from several hardware and software companies. Internships and summer jobs with such corporations are always beneficial and provide experience that will give you the edge over your competition. General computer job fairs are also held throughout the year in larger cities. Some job openings are advertised in newspapers. There are many online career sites listed on the World Wide Web that post job openings, salary surveys, and current employment trends. The Web also has online publications that deal specifically with quality assurance. You can also obtain information from associations for quality professionals, such as the Quality Assurance Institute, and from computer organizations, including the IEEE Computer Society.

Advancement

Quality assurance testers are considered entry-level positions in some companies. After acquiring more experience and technical knowledge, testers might become quality assurance analysts, who write and revise the quality assurance standards or specifications for new programs. They also create the quality assurance examinations that testers use to evaluate programs. This usually involves using computer programming. Some analysts also evaluate proposals for new software products to decide whether the proposed product is capable of doing what it is supposed to do. Analysts are sometimes promoted to *quality assurance manager* positions, which requires some knowledge of software coding, the entire software production process, and test automation. Quality assurance managers direct quality assurance teams for specific software products before and beyond their release.

Some testers also go on to become programmers or software engineers.

Earnings

Full-time, entry-level quality assurance testers initially earn $25,000 to $43,000 or more per year, depending on the location and size of the company. Testers with degrees who have worked in the industry for less than 10 years usually make approximately $49,000 to $53,000 per year. High-end salaries for those with many years of technical and management experience can reach $60,000 or higher. Testers also generally receive a full benefits package as well, including health insurance, paid vacation, and sick leave. As in many other industries, people with advanced degrees have the potential to make the most money.

Work Environment

Quality assurance testers work in computer labs or offices. The work is generally repetitive and even monotonous. If a game is being tested, for example, a tester may have to play it for hours until it finally crashes, if it does at all. This might seem like great fun, but most testers agree that even the newest, most exciting game loses its appeal after several hours. This aspect of the job proves to be very frustrating and boring for some individuals.

Since quality assurance work involves keeping very detailed records, the job can also be stressful. For example, if a tester works on a word processing program for several hours, he or she must be able to recall at any moment the last few keystrokes entered—in case the program crashes. This requires long periods of concentration, which can be tiring. Monitoring computer screens to make sure automated quality assurance tests are running properly often has the same effect.

Meeting with supervisors, programmers, and engineers to discuss ideas for the software projects can be intellectually stimulating. In these situations, testers should feel at ease communicating with superiors. On the other end, testers who field customer complaints on the telephone may be forced to bear the brunt of customer dissatisfaction, an almost certain source of stress.

Quality assurance testers generally work regular, 40-hour weeks. During the final stages before a program goes into mass production and packaging, however, testers are frequently called on to work overtime.

Outlook

The number of positions in the field of quality assurance is expected to grow faster than the average through 2006, according to the U.S. Department of Labor. This trend is predicted despite an increasing level of quality assurance automation. Before, software companies were able to make big profits by being the first to introduce a specific kind of product, such as a word processor or presentation kit, to the marketplace. Now, with so many versions of similar software on the market, competition is forcing firms to focus their energies on customer service. Many companies, therefore, aim to perfect their software applications before they hit the shelves. Searching for every small program glitch requires the effort of a lot of quality assurance testers.

This same push toward premarket perfection helps explain the development of more accurate and efficient quality assurance automation. To stay competitive, companies must refine their quality assurance procedures to ever-higher levels. "In the next few years, testing will begin on Day One of the project," says Steve. "This means that testers will be involved in the process from the beginning because they are the ones who know what the product's functionality should be. Without testing requirements, you cannot do anything."

For More Information

For information on the certified quality analyst, certified software test engineer, and certified assessor certifications, contact:

Quality Assurance Institute
7575 Dr. Phillips Boulevard, Suite 350
Orlando, FL 32819
Tel: 407-363-1111
Web: http://www.qaiusa.com

Software Designers

Overview

Software designers are responsible for creating new ideas and designing prepackaged and customized computer software. Software designers devise applications, such as word processors, front-end database programs, and spreadsheets, that make it possible for computers to complete given tasks and to solve problems. Once a need in the market has been identified, software designers first conceive of the program on a global level by outlining what the program will do. Then they write the specifications from which programmers code computer commands to perform the given functions.

History

The first major advances in modern computer technology were made during World War II. After the war, it was thought that the enormous size of computers, which easily took up the space of entire warehouses, would limit their use to huge government projects, such as processing the U.S. census, for example.

The introduction of semiconductors to computer technology made possible smaller and less-expensive computers. Businesses began adapting computers to their operations as early as 1954. Within 30 years, computers had revolutionized the way people work, play, and shop. Today, computers are everywhere, from the business world, to government agencies, charitable organizations, and private homes. Over the years, technology has continued to shrink computer size and increase computer speed at an unprecedented rate.

"In 1983, software development exploded with the introduction of the personal computer. Standard applications included not only spreadsheets and word processors, but graphics packages and communications systems," according to "Events in the History of Computing," compiled by the IEEE Computer Society.

Advances in computer technology have enabled professionals to put computers to work in a range of activities once thought impossible. Computer software designers have been able to take advantage of computer hardware improvements in speed, memory capacity, reliability, and accuracy to create programs to do just about anything. With the extensive proliferation of computers in our society, there is a great market for user-friendly, imaginative, and high-performance software. Business and industry rely heavily on the power of computers and use both prepackaged software and software that has been custom designed for its own specific use. Also, with more people purchasing computer systems for home use, the retail market for prepackaged software has grown steadily. Given these conditions, computer software designing will be an important field in the industry for years to come.

The software industry is comprised of many facets, including personal computer packaged applications (known as "shrink-wrapped software"); operating systems for stand-alone and networked systems; management tools for networks; enterprise software that enables efficient management of large corporations' production, sales, and information systems; software applications and operating systems for mainframe computers; and customized software for specific industry management, according to the Software Publishers Association (SPA).

Packaged software is written for mass distribution, not for the specific needs of a particular user. Broad categories include operating systems, utilities, applications, and programming languages. Operating systems, according to the SPA, control the basic functions of a computer or network. Utilities perform support functions, such as backup or virus protection. Programming software is used to develop the sets of instructions that build all other types of software. The software that most computer users are familiar with is called *application software*. This category includes word-processing, spreadsheets, and email packages commonly used in business as well as games and reference software that is used in homes, and subject- or skill-based software that is used in schools.

The Job

Without software, computer hardware would have nothing to do. Computers need to be told exactly what to do. Software is the set of codes that gives the computer those instructions. It comes in the form of the familiar prepackaged software that you find in a computer store, such as games, word processing programs, spreadsheets, and desktop publishing programs, and in a customized application designed to fit the specific need of a particular business. Software designers are the initiators of these complex programs. *Computer programmers* then create the software by writing the code that carries out the directives of the designer.

Software designers must envision every detail of what an application will do, how it will do it, and how it will look (the user interface). A simple example is how a home accounting program is created. The software designer first lays out the overall functionality of the program, specifying what it should be able to do, such as balancing a checkbook, keeping track of incoming and outgoing bills, and maintaining records of expenses. For each of these tasks, the software designer will outline the design detail for the specific functions that he or she has mandated, such as what menus and icons will be used, what each screen will look like, and whether there will be help or dialog boxes to assist the user. For example, the designer may specify that the expense record part of the program produce a pie chart that shows the percentage of each household expense in the overall household budget. The designer can specify that the program automatically display the pie chart each time a budget assessment is completed or only after the user clicks on the appropriate icon on the toolbar.

Some software companies specialize in building custom-designed software. This software is highly specialized for specific needs or problems of particular businesses. Some businesses are large enough that they employ in-house software designers who create software applications for their computer systems. A related field is *software engineering,* which involves writing customized complex software to solve a specific engineering or technical problem of a business or industry.

Whether the designer is working on a mass-market or a custom application, the first step is to define the overall goals for the application. This is typically done in consultation with management if the software designer is working at a software supply company, or with the client if the designer is working on a custom-designed project. Then, the software designer studies the goals and problems of the project. If working on custom-designed software, the designer must also take into consideration the existing computer system of the client. Next, the software designer works on the program strategy and specific design detail that he or she has envisioned. At this point, the designer may need to write a proposal outlining the design and estimating time and cost allocations. Based on this report, management or the client decides if the project should proceed.

Once approval is given, the software designer and the programmers begin working on writing the software program. Typically, the software designer writes the specifications for the program, and the *applications programmers* write the programming codes.

In addition to the design detail duties, a software designer may be responsible for writing a user's manual or at least writing a report for what should be included in the user's manual. After testing and debugging the program, the software designer will present it to management or to the client.

Requirements

High School

High school students interested in computer science should take as many computer, math, and science courses as possible since they provide fundamental math and computer knowledge and teach analytical thinking skills. Classes that rely on schematic drawing and flowcharts are also very valuable. English and speech courses help students improve their communications skills, which are very important to software designers who must make formal presentations to management and clients. Also, many technical/vocational schools offer programs in software programming and design. The qualities developed by these classes, plus imagination and an ability to work well under pressure, are key to success in software design.

Postsecondary Training

A bachelor's degree in computer science plus one year's experience with a programming language is required for most software designers.

In the past, the computer industry has tended to be pretty flexible about official credentials; demonstrated computer proficiency and work experience have often been enough to obtain a good position. However, as more people enter the field, competition increases, and job requirements become more stringent. Technical knowledge alone does not suffice in the field of software design. The successful software designer should have at least peripheral knowledge of the field for which he or she intends to design software, such as business, education, or science. An individual with a bachelor's degree in computer science with a minor in business or accounting has an excellent chance for employment in designing business/accounting software, for example. " . . . [I]ncreasingly, computer professionals need to be very good in business," says David Weldon, senior editor in charge of *Computerworld's* Information Technology careers coverage, in the article "Scoring the Best Tech Jobs," by Susan Gregory Thomas, on *U.S. News Online.* "I have a stack of resumes three feet high of rejects, and it's not because these candidates didn't have technical backgrounds," says Andrew Popell, cofounder of Harvest Technology, a software company that develops applications for portfolio managers in the financial industry, in the same article. Another example of this is that those with degrees in education and subsequent teaching experience are much sought after as designers for educational software.

Other Requirements

Software design is project- and detail-oriented, and therefore software designers must be patient and diligent. They must also enjoy problem-solving challenges and be able to work under a deadline with minimal supervision. Software designers should also possess good communications skills for consulting both with management and with clients who will have varying levels of technical expertise.

Software companies are looking for individuals with vision and imagination to help them create new and exciting programs to sell in the ever-competitive software market. Superior technical skills and knowledge combined with motivation, imagination, and exuberance make an attractive candidate.

Exploring

Spending a day with a working software designer or applications programmer will allow you to experience firsthand what this work entails. School guidance counselors can often help you organize such a meeting.

If you are interested in computer industry careers in general, you should learn as much as possible about computers. You should keep up with new technology by reading computer magazines and by talking to other computer users. You should join computer clubs and use online services and the Internet for information about this field.

Advanced students can put their design/programming knowledge to work by designing and programming their own applications, such as simple games and utility programs.

Employers

Software designers are employed throughout the United States. Opportunities are best in large cities and suburbs where business and industry are active. Programmers who develop software systems work for software manufacturers, many of whom are in Silicon Valley, in northern California. There are also concentrations of software manufacturers in Boston, Chicago, and Atlanta, among other places. Designers who adapt and tailor the software to meet specific needs of end-users work for those end-user companies, many of which are scattered across the country.

Starting Out

Software design positions are regarded as some of the most interesting, and therefore the most competitive, in the computer industry. Some software designers are promoted from an entry-level programming position. Software design positions in software supply companies and large custom software companies will be difficult to secure straight out of college or technical/vocational school.

Entry-level programming and design jobs may be listed in the help wanted sections of newspapers. Employment agencies and online job banks are other good sources.

Students in technical schools or universities should take advantage of the campus placement office. They should check regularly for internship postings, job listings, and notices of on-campus recruitment. Placement offices are also valuable resources for resume tips and interviewing techniques. Internships and summer jobs with such corporations are always beneficial and provide experience that will give you the edge over your competition. General computer job fairs are also held throughout the year in larger cities.

There are many online career sites listed on the World Wide Web that post job openings, salary surveys, and current employment trends. The Web also has online publications that deal specifically with computer jobs. Interested students can obtain information from various computer organizations. Because this is such a competitive field, applicants will need to show initiative and creativity that will set them apart from other applicants.

Advancement

In general, programmers work between one and five years before being promoted to software designer. A programmer can move up by demonstrating an ability to create new software ideas that translate well into marketable applications. Individuals with a knack for spotting trends in the software market are also likely to advance.

Those software designers who demonstrate leadership may be promoted to *project team leader*. Project team leaders are responsible for developing new software projects and overseeing the work done by software designers and applications programmers. With experience as a project team leader, a motivated software designer may be promoted to a position as a *software manager* who runs projects from an even higher level.

The key to advancement in software design is keeping up-to-date with changing technology. A career in the computer industry means that education never stops. For advancement as a software designer, it means not only keeping up with advances in computer technology, it means making the changes happen.

Earnings

Salaries for software designers vary with the size of the company and with location. Salaries may be slightly higher in areas where there is a large concentration of computer companies, such as the Silicon Valley in northern California and parts of Washington, Oregon, and the East Coast.

Software designers' salaries range from $38,000 for a beginning designer to $51,000 for a senior designer or project team leader. At the managerial level, salaries are even higher and can reach $75,000+.

Most designers work for large companies, which offer full benefits packages that include health insurance, vacation and sick time, profit sharing, and retirement plans.

Work Environment

Software designers work in comfortable environments. Many computer companies are known for their casual work atmosphere; employees generally do not have to wear suits, except during client meetings. Overall, software designers work standard weeks. However, they may be required to work overtime when a deadline is near. It is common in software design to share office or cubical space with two or three co-workers, which is typical of the team approach to working. A software designer or applications programmer spends much of the day in front of the computer, although a software designer will have occasional team meetings or meetings with clients.

Software design can be stressful work for several reasons. First, the market for software is very competitive and companies are pushing to develop more innovative software and to get it on the market before the competitors. For this same reason, software design is also very exciting and creative work. Second, software designers are given a project and a deadline. It is up to the designer and team members to budget their time to finish in the allocated time. Finally, working with programming languages and so many details can be very frustrating, especially when the tiniest glitch means the program will not run. For this reason, software designers must be patient and diligent.

Outlook

Jobs in software design are expected to grow faster than the average through the year 2006, according to the *Occupational Outlook Handbook*. Employment of computing professionals is expected to increase much faster than average as technology becomes more sophisticated and organizations continue to adopt and integrate these technologies, making for plentiful job openings. Hardware designers and systems programmers are constantly developing faster, more powerful, and more user-friendly hardware and operating systems. As long as these advancements continue, the industry will need software designers to create software to use these improvements.

Growth rates for the packaged software industry have been extremely vigorous through the 1990s, with an average growth rate of 12 percent per year. Experts are projecting an approximate 10 percent annual growth for software.

Business may have less need to contract for custom software as more prepackaged software, which allows users with minimal computer skills to "build" their own software using components that they customize themselves, arrives on the market. However, the growth in the retail software market is expected to make up for this loss in customized services.

The expanding integration of Internet technologies by businesses has resulted in a rising demand for skilled professionals who can develop and support a variety of Internet applications.

For More Information

Contact ACM for information on internships, student membership, and the ACM student magazine, Crossroads. *ACM also offers a student Web site at* http://www.acm.org/membership/student/.

Association for Computing Machinery
1515 Broadway
New York, NY 10036-5701
Tel: 212-869-7440
Email: SIGS@acm.org
Web: http://www.acm.org

Software Engineers

Computer science Mathematics	School Subjects
Mechanical/manipulative Technical/scientific	Personal Skills
Primarily indoors Primarily one location	Work Environment
Bachelor's degree	Minimum Education Level
$39,722 to $50,000 to $80,000+	Salary Range
Recommended	Certification or Licensing
Much faster than the average	Outlook

Overview

Software engineers are responsible for customizing existing software programs to meet the needs and desires of a particular business or industry. First, they spend considerable time researching, defining, and analyzing the problem at hand. Then, they develop software programs to resolve the problem on the computer. There are over 216,000 computer engineers employed in the United States.

History

The first major advances in modern computer technology were made during World War II. After the war, it was thought that the enormous size of computers, which easily took up the space of entire warehouses, would limit their use to huge government projects. Accordingly, the 1950 census was computer processed.

The introduction of semiconductors to computer technology made possible smaller and less expensive computers. Businesses began adapting computers to their operations as early as 1954. Within 30 years, computers had revolutionized the way people work, play, and go shopping. Today, computers are everywhere, from businesses of all kinds, to government agencies, charitable organizations, and private homes. Over the years, technology has continued to shrink computer size and increase computer speed at an unprecedented rate.

Advances in computer technology have enabled professionals to put computers to work in a range of activities once thought impossible. In the past several years, computer software engineers have been able to take advantage of computer hardware improvements in speed, memory capacity, reliability, and accuracy to create programs that do just about anything. Computer engineering blossomed as a distinct subfield in the computer industry after the new performance levels were achieved. This relative lateness is explained by the fact that the programs written by software engineers to solve business and scientific problems are very intricate and complex, requiring a lot of computing power. Although many computer scientists will continue to focus research on further developing hardware, the emphasis in the field has moved more squarely to software. Given this change, computer engineering will be an important field in the industry for years to come.

The Job

Every day, businesses, scientists, and government agencies encounter difficult problems that they cannot solve manually, either because the problem is just too complicated or because it would take too much time to calculate the appropriate solutions. For example, astronomers receive thousands of pieces of data every hour from probes and satellites in space as well as telescopes here on earth. If they had to process the information themselves, that is, compile careful comparisons with previous years' readings, look for patterns or cycles, and keep accurate records of the origin of the various data, a project would be so cumbersome and lengthy as to make it next to impossible. Astronomers can, however, process such data, but only thanks to the extensive help of computers. Computer software engineers define and analyze specific problems in business or science and help develop computer software applications that effectively solve them. The software engineers that work in the field of astronomy are well versed in its concepts, but many other kinds of software engineers exist as well.

The basic structure of computer engineering is the same in any industry. First, software engineers research specific problems and investigate ways in which computers can be programmed to perform certain functions. Then, they develop software applications customized to the needs and desires of the business or organization. For example, many software engineers work with the federal government and insurance companies to develop new ways of reducing paperwork, such as income tax returns, claims forms, and applications. There are currently several independent but major form automation projects taking place throughout the United States. As software engineers find new ways to solve the problems associated with form automation, more forms are completed online and fewer on paper.

Software engineers specializing in a particular industry, such as a particular science, business, or medicine, are expected to demonstrate a certain level of proficiency in that industry. Consequently, the specific nature of their work varies from project to project and industry to industry. Software engineers also differ by the nature of their employer. Some work for consulting firms that complete software projects for different clients on an individual basis. Others work for large companies that hire engineers full time to develop software customized to their needs. Software engineering professionals also differ by level of responsibility. *Software engineering technicians* assist engineers in completing projects. They are usually knowledgeable in analog, digital, and microprocessor electronics and programming techniques. Technicians know enough about program design and computer languages to fill in details left out by engineers or programmers, who conceive of the program from a large-scale perspective. Technicians might also test new software applications with special diagnostic equipment.

Software engineering is extremely detail-oriented work. Since computers do only what they are programmed to do, engineers have to account for every bit of information with a programming command. Software engineers are thus required to be very well organized and precise. In order to achieve this, they generally follow strict procedures in completing an assignment.

First, they interview clients and colleagues in order to determine exactly what they want the final program to be able to do. Defining the problem by outlining the goal can sometimes be difficult, especially when clients have little technical training. Then, software engineers evaluate the software applications already in use by the client to understand how and why they are failing to fulfill the needs of the operation. After this period of fact-gathering, the engineers use methods of scientific analysis and mathematical models to develop possible solutions to the problems. These analytical methods allow them to predict and measure the outcomes of different proposed designs.

When they have developed a good notion of what type of program is required to fulfill the client's needs, they draw up a detailed proposal that includes estimates of time and cost allocations. Management must then decide if the project will meet their needs, if it is a good investment, and whether it will be undertaken.

Once a proposal is accepted, both software engineers and technicians begin work on the project. They verify with hardware engineers that the proposed software program can be completed with existing hardware systems. Typically, the engineer writes program specifications and the technician uses his or her knowledge of computer languages to write preliminary programming. Engineers focus most of their efforts on program strategies, testing procedures, and reviewing technicians' work.

Software engineers are usually responsible for a significant amount of technical writing, including projects proposals, progress reports, and user manuals. They are required to meet regularly with clients in order to keep project goals clear and to learn about any changes as quickly as possible.

When the program is completed, the software engineer organizes a demonstration of the final product to the client. Supervisors, management, and users are generally present. Some software engineers may offer to install the program, train users on it, and make arrangements for ongoing technical support.

Requirements

A high school diploma is the minimum requirement for software engineering technicians. A bachelor's or advanced degree in computer science or engineering is required for most software engineers.

High School

High school students interested in pursuing this career should take as many computer, math, and science courses as possible since they provide fundamental math and computer knowledge and teach analytical thinking skills. Classes that rely on schematic drawing and flowcharts are also very valuable. English and speech courses help students improve their communications skills, which are very important for software engineers.

Postsecondary Training

There are several ways to enter the field of software engineering, although it is becoming increasingly necessary to pursue formal postsecondary education. Individuals without an associate's degree may first be hired in the quality assurance or technical support departments of a company. Many complete associate degrees while working and then are promoted into software engineering technician positions. As more and more well-educated professionals enter the industry, however, it is becoming more important for applicants to have at least an associate's degree in computer engineering or programming. Many technical and vocational schools offer a variety of programs that prepare students for jobs as software engineering technicians.

Interested students should consider carefully their long-range goals. Being promoted from a technician's job to that of software engineer often requires a bachelor's degree. In the past, the computer industry has tended to be fairly flexible about official credentials; demonstrated computer proficiency and work experience have often been enough to obtain a good position. This may hold true for some in the future. The majority of young computer professionals entering the field for the first time, however, will be college educated. Therefore, those with no formal education or work experience will have less chance of employment.

Obtaining a postsecondary degree in computer engineering is usually considered challenging and even difficult. In addition to natural ability, students should be hard working and determined to succeed. Software engineers planning to work in specific technical fields, such as medicine, law, or business, should receive some formal training in that particular discipline.

Certification or Licensing

Another option for individuals interested in software engineering is to pursue commercial certification. Certification programs are usually run by computer companies that wish to train professionals in working with their products. Classes are challenging and examinations can be rigorous. New programs are introduced every year.

Other Requirements

Software engineers need strong communications skills in order to be able to make formal business presentations and interact with people having different levels of computer expertise. They must also be detail oriented and work well under pressure.

Earnings

Software engineering technicians usually earn beginning salaries of $24,000. Computer engineers with a bachelor's degree in computer engineering earned starting salaries of $39,722 in 1997, according to the *Occupational Outlook Handbook*. New computer engineers with a master's degree averaged $44,734, and those with a Ph.D. averaged $63,367. Software engineers generally earn more in geographical areas where there are clusters of computer companies, such as the Silicon Valley in northern California.

Experienced software engineers can earn over $80,000 a year. When they are promoted into management, as project team leaders or software managers, they earn even more.

Most software engineers work for companies that offer extensive benefits, including health insurance, sick leave, and paid vacation. In some smaller computer companies, however, benefits may be limited.

Work Environment

Software engineers generally work in comfortable office environments. Overall, they usually work 40-hour weeks, but this depends on the nature of the employer and the expertise of the engineer. In consulting firms, for example, it is typical for engineers to work long hours and to frequently travel to out-of-town assignments.

Software engineers generally receive an assignment and a time frame within which to accomplish it; daily work details are often left up to the individuals. Some engineers work relatively lightly at the beginning of a project but work a lot of overtime at the end in order to catch up. Most engineers are not compensated for overtime. Software engineering can be stressful, especially when working to meet deadlines. Working with programming languages and intense details is often frustrating. Therefore, software engineers should be patient, enjoy problem-solving challenges, and work well under pressure.

Outlook

The field of software engineering is expected to be one of the fastest growing occupations through the year 2006, according to the U.S. Department of Labor. Demands made on computers increase every day and from all industries. The development of one kind of software sparks ideas for many others. In addition, users rely on software programs that are increasingly user-friendly.

Since technology changes so rapidly, software engineers are advised to keep up on the latest developments. While the need for software engineers will remain high, computer languages will probably change every few years. Software engineers will need to attend seminars and workshops to learn new computer languages and software design. They also should read trade magazines, surf the Internet, and talk with colleagues about the field. Continuing education helps ensure that software engineers are well equipped to meet the needs of the workplace.

For More Information

For more information on careers in computer software, contact:

Software & Information Industry Association
1730 M Street, NW, Suite 700
Washington, DC 20036-4510
Tel: 202-452-1600
Web: http://www.siia.net

For certification information, contact:

Institute for Certification of Computing Professionals
2200 East Devon Avenue, Suite 247
Des Plaines, IL 60018
Tel: 847-299-4227
Web: http://www.iccp.org

Systems Set Up Specialists

Business Computer science	School Subjects
Mechanical/manipulative Technical/scientific	Personal Skills
Primarily indoors Primarily one location	Work Environment
High school diploma	Minimum Education Level
$26,130 to $32,300 to $40,000	Salary Range
None available	Certification or Licensing
Faster than the average	Outlook

Overview

Systems set up specialists are responsible for installing new computer systems and upgrading existing ones to meet the specifications of the client. They install hardware, such as memory, sound cards, fax/modems, fans, microprocessors, and systems boards. They also load software and configure the hard drive appropriately. Some systems set up specialists install computer systems at the client's location. Installation might include making normal hard drive or network server configurations as well as connecting peripherals like printers, phones, fax machines, modems, and terminals. They might also be involved with technical support in providing initial training to users. Systems set up specialists are employed by computer manufacturing companies or computer service companies nationwide, or they may be employed as part of the technical support department of many businesses. Systems set up specialists are sometimes called *technical support technicians, desktop analyst/specialists,* and *PC set up specialists.*

History

The first major advances in modern computer technology were made during World War II. After the war, it was thought that the enormous size of computers, which easily took up the space of entire warehouses, would limit their use to huge government projects. Accordingly, the 1950 census was computer processed.

The introduction of semiconductors to computer technology made smaller and less expensive computers possible. Businesses began adapting computers to their operations as early as 1954. Within 30 years, computers had revolutionized the way people work, play, and shop. Today, computers are everywhere, from businesses of all kinds, to government agencies, charitable organizations, and private homes. Over the years, technology has continued to shrink computer size and increase computer speed at an unprecedented rate.

Several big companies, such as IBM, Apple, Microsoft, and Intel, have been the driving force behind various stages of the computer revolution. As technology advances, however, new companies spring up to compete with them. For example, IBM's first competitive challenge came when other companies decided to produce IBM-compatible PC clones. Today, the market for computers is saturated with different brands offering similar features. As a result, many companies are attempting to distinguish themselves from the competition by providing extra service to clients. Offering customized hardware and software is one way for them to do this. Systems set up specialists, therefore, are a very important part of the selling process. They make sure that clients receive exactly what they need and want. If the computer system is not set up correctly to begin with, clients might take their business elsewhere in the future. As competition in the computer industry grows even fiercer, the customer service roles of systems set up specialists will become even more important.

The Job

Most businesses and organizations use computers on a daily basis. In fact, it is very difficult to find an office or store that does not use computer technology to help with at least one business task. One thing is for sure—there are so many different ways in which a business or individual can use computer technology that it would be impossible to count them. The wide variety could translate into big problems for computer companies if they tried to sell identical computer systems to every client. For example, a freelance writer would probably not be interested in a math card used for advanced mathematical calculations on personal computers. Likewise, a bank or insurance company has different database needs than a law firm.

In order to meet the various needs of clients, many computer manufacturers, retailers, and service centers offer to customize commercial hardware and software for each client. Systems might differ by quantity of RAM (random access memory), speed and type of fax/modem, networking capabilities, and software packages. Systems set up specialists are responsible for installing new computer systems and upgrading existing ones to meet the specifications of the client. The main differences among set up specialists are their clients (individuals or businesses) and the level of systems they are qualified to work on.

Some specialists work in-house for large computer manufactures, retailers, or service centers. Their clients are typically individuals buying for home use as well as small- to medium-size businesses with minimal computing needs.

In the set up lab, specialists receive orders that list system specifications. Then, they follow instructions on how to set up the computer properly. They install hardware, such as memory chips, sound cards, fax/modems, fans, microprocessors, and system boards. They also install any software packages requested by the client. Next, they configure the hard drive so it knows exactly what hardware and software is connected to it. Finally, they run diagnostic tests on the system to make sure everything is running well.

The main goal is to eliminate the need for clients to do any set up work on the computer once they receive it. Clients should be able to plug it in, turn it on, and get it to work right away. In some cases, specialists will be sent to a client's location to install the system and provide some initial training on how to use it.

Other systems set up specialists work for companies that sell predominately to medium- and large-sized businesses. These specialists split their time between the employer's set up lab and the client's location. In the lab, they make initial preparations for installation. Some of the computer equipment might come from other manufacturers or suppliers, and systems set up specialists have to verify that it is free of defects. They also check that they have all the necessary hardware parts, software packages, etc. before going to the client's location.

Depending on the size and complexity of the system to be installed, specialists might travel to the client's location one or more times before installation in order to map out the required wiring, communications lines, and space. It is very important to plan these details carefully. If wires are hard to reach, for example, future repairs and upgrades will be difficult. If the system is really big, set up specialists might recommend and build a raised floor in the client's computer center. The paneled floor allows easy access to the complex electrical and communications wiring.

Once thorough preparations have been made, set up specialists move the equipment to the clients' location to begin installation. Their on-site work might include configuring hard drives or network servers. They also connect peripherals, such as printers, phones, fax machines, modems, and numerous networked terminals. When everything is in place, they run extensive diagnostic tests in order to ensure that the system is running well. Invariably, they encounter problems. One terminal may not be able to send files to another, for example. Another might be unable to establish fax communications outside the company. Solving problems requires consulting flow charts, other computer professionals, and technical manuals. The next round of testing occurs when the users begin working on the system. Some clients might prefer to simulate normal use while set up specialists stand by to correct problems. Large business installations can take days or even weeks to complete.

Sometimes, set up specialists are involved with technical support in training client users on the new system. They have to be well versed in the details of how to use the system properly and be able to explain them to individuals who might not know a lot about computers.

Requirements

High School

If this industry interests you, try to take any mechanics and electronics classes that focus on understanding how complex machinery works. These classes will introduce you to the basics of reading flow charts and schematic drawings and understanding technical documents. The ability to read these documents efficiently and accurately is a prerequisite for computer set up work. Don't forget to take computer classes, especially those that explain the basic functioning of computer technology. English and speech classes will also help you build your communications skills—another important quality since set up specialists often work closely with many different people.

Postsecondary Training

A high school diploma is a minimum educational requirement for most systems set up specialist positions. However, the competitive nature of this industry is increasing the importance of postsecondary education, such as an associate's degree. Computer technology is advancing so rapidly that without a solid understanding of the basics, set up specialists cannot keep up with the changes. Also, many aspiring computer professionals use system set up positions as a springboard to higher-level jobs in the company. Formal computer education, along with work experience, gives them a better chance for advancement.

Other Requirements

Do you work well with your hands? Manual work is performed on large and small scales—sometimes thick cables and communications lines must be installed; other times tiny memory chips or microprocessors are needed. Therefore, you'll need to demonstrate good manual dexterity.

You should also be curious about how things work. Systems set up specialists are typically the kind of people who tinker around the house on VCRs, televisions, small appliances, and computers. Genuine curiosity of this type is important because you'll constantly be challenged to learn about new equipment and technologies. When things go wrong during installation, you will be called on to become electronic and computer problem-solvers and so you must be prepared with a solid understanding of the basics.

Exploring

There are several ways to obtain a better understanding of what it is like to be a set up specialist. One way is to try to organize a career day through school or friends and relatives. In this way, you could spend a day on the job with set up specialists and experience firsthand what the work entails.

You might also want to work part time for a computer repair shop. Repair shops usually do many upgrades that involve the installation of new hardware, like faster modems and microprocessors and more memory. Working in such a shop after school or on weekends will give you the opportunity to observe or practice the precision work of a set up specialist.

Depending on your level of computer knowledge, you may want to volunteer to set up new personal computers for friends or charitable organizations in your neighborhood. What about installing software or customizing some features of the operating system to better meet the needs of the user?

Employers

In the early days of the computer industry, many jobs were clustered around northern California, where many of the big computer companies were headquartered. This is no longer true. Many top computer companies are located throughout the United States, and with them come a number of employment opportunities. Some computer hardware powerhouses include Dell, Hewlett-Packard, and IBM. Many mid- to small-sized companies may not have the need for a specific department devoted to computer setup. In such situations, other computer professionals may be assigned setup duties besides their regular job descriptions.

A number of jobs may also be found with smaller companies that contract their services to retail stores or offer them directly to the public. Services may include hardware and software installation, upgrading, and repair.

Starting Out

Most positions in systems set up are considered entry level. If you plan to enter this field without a postsecondary education but with computer skills and experience, you will need to network with working computer professionals for potential employment opportunities. Jobs are advertised in the newspaper every week; in fact, many papers devote entire sections to computer-related positions. Also, don't forget the benefits of working with employment agencies. Another job-hunting technique is to conduct online searches on the World Wide Web. Many computer companies post employment opportunities and accept resumes and applications online.

If you plan to enter the field by completing an advanced degree, say an associate's degree in computer technology, for example, work closely with your school's placement office. Many firms looking for computer professionals inform schools first since they are assured of meeting candidates with a certain level of proficiency in the field.

Advancement

Within systems set up, there are several ways specialists can be promoted. One is by working on increasingly complex systems installations. Another is by having supervisory or managerial responsibility for the set up department. Other specialists choose to pursue promotion in different functional areas, such as technical support, computer engineering, or systems analysis.

When set up specialists demonstrate strong ability and drive, they are often assigned to larger and more complex installations. Instead of installing commercial software, for example, the specialist might now be responsible for constructing flowcharts or other drawings as part of the overall installation plan. Also, a specialist who at first works on relatively small departmental networks might be asked to work on company-wide networks.

Computer professionals who use systems set up as a springboard to other positions usually have formal education in a certain field, such as software or hardware engineering, for example. They seek promotion by keeping an eye on job openings within their respective fields.

If specialists show leadership ability, they might be promoted to supervisory and then managerial positions. These positions require more administrative duties and less hands-on work. For example, supervisors are usually in charge of scheduling installation jobs and assigning different jobs to various individuals, taking into account their levels of expertise and experience. With more formal education, managers might be involved with the strategic planning of a computer company, deciding what level of service the company is willing to offer to clients.

Specialists may also decide to start their own computer businesses. Many office supply and electronics stores contract with area computer companies to provide customers with services such as set up and installation, upgrading, and technical support. If this career path is appealing, educate yourself in the basics of operating a small business, such as accounting, marketing, or inventory.

Earnings

According to a 1997 Technical Support Salary Survey, systems set up specialists with entry-level customer service responsibilities earned an annual average of $26,130; those with experience earned an averaged annual salary of about $32,300. Senior set up specialists with superior technical skills and work experience earned an average salary of about $40,000. Computer professionals typically earn more in areas where there are clusters of computer companies, like northern California and parts of the East Coast. However the high cost of living in these areas may offset the benefits of a higher salary.

Most full-time set up specialists work for companies that provide a full range of benefits, including health insurance, sick leave, and paid vacation. In addition, many employers offer tuition reimbursement programs to employees who successfully complete course work in the field. Set up specialists who operate their own businesses are responsible for providing their own benefits.

Work Environment

Systems set up specialists work primarily indoors, in a comfortable environment. This is not a desk job; specialists move around a lot either in the lab or at the client site. Travel to client locations is required for many set up specialists. The work also requires some lifting of heavy machinery, which can be avoided if an individual physically cannot perform this task. Given the nature of the work, dress is casual, although those who install systems at the client's site must be dressed in presentable business attire.

Set up specialists usually work a regular 40-hour week. However, they might be asked to work overtime when big installations are reaching final phases. They might have to work during off-hours if the client requires installation to be done then.

Installation work can be tedious. There are many details involving wiring, communications, and configurations. Set up specialists must therefore be patient and thorough, which can be frustrating at times. When problems arise, they must work well under stress and be able to think clearly about how to resolve the issues. If set up specialists are also involved in user training, they must communicate clearly and be understanding of others' problems.

Outlook

The demand for systems set up specialists is expected to grow faster than the average through 2006, according to the *Occupational Outlook Handbook*. Most jobs in the computer industry, especially those that provide a special or unique service to computer customers, will enjoy increased demand.

The ability to network and share information within the company allows businesses to be productive and work more efficiently. As new technology is developed, companies may upgrade, or replace their systems altogether. Skilled workers will be in demand by companies to staff their technical support departments and provide services ranging from set up and installation to diagnostics.

Also, because of falling hardware and software prices, it has become more affordable for consumers to purchase home computer setups. Although advances in software technology have made program installation easy, computer companies will continue to offer installation services as a way to win customers from competitors. In addition, fierce competition will push companies to provide increasingly specialized services in terms of customization of computer systems. As computers become more sophisticated, highly trained set up specialists will be needed to install them correctly. It will therefore be very important for set up specialists to stay up to date with technological advances through continuing education, seminars, or work training.

For More Information

For information regarding industry salary expectations or employment opportunities nationwide, contact:

Association of Support Professionals
17 Main Street
Watertown, MA 02172-4491
Tel: 617-924-3944, ext. 14
Web: http://www.asponline.com/

Technical Support Specialists

	School Subjects
Computer science English Mathematics	

	Personal Skills
Helping/teaching Technical/scientific	

	Work Environment
Primarily indoors Primarily one location	

	Minimum Education Level
High school diploma	

	Salary Range
$25,000 to $36,500 to $50,000+	

	Certification or Licensing
Voluntary	

	Outlook
Much faster than the average	

Overview

Technical support specialists investigate and resolve problems in computer functioning. They listen to customer complaints, walk customers through possible solutions, and write technical reports based on these events. Technical support specialists have different duties depending on whom they assist and what they fix. Regardless of specialty, all technical support specialists must be very knowledgeable about the products with which they work and be able to communicate effectively with users from different technical backgrounds. They must be patient with frustrated users and be able to perform well under stress. Technical support is basically like solving mysteries, so support specialists should enjoy the challenge of problem solving and have strong analytical thinking skills.

History

The first major advances in modern computer technology were made during World War II. After the war, it was thought that the enormous size of computers, which easily took up the space of entire warehouses, would limit their use to huge government projects. The 1950 census, for example, was computer processed.

The introduction of semiconductors to computer technology made possible smaller and less expensive computers. Businesses began adapting computers to their operations as early as 1954. Within 30 years, computers had revolutionized the way people work, play, and go shopping. Today, computers are everywhere, from businesses of all kinds to government agencies, charitable organizations, and private homes. Over the years, technology has continued to shrink computer size and increase computer speed at an unprecedented rate.

Technical support has been around since the development of the first computers for the simple reason that, like all other machines, computers always experience problems at one time or another. Several market phenomena explain the increase in demand for competent technical support specialists. First of all, as more and more companies enter the computer hardware, software, and peripheral markets, the intense competition to win customers has resulted in many companies offering free or reasonably priced technical support as part of the purchase package. A company uses its reputation and the availability of a technical support department to differentiate its products from those of other companies, even though the tangible products, such as a hard drive, may actually be physically identical. Second, personal computers (PCs) have entered private homes in large numbers, and the sheer quantity of users has risen so dramatically that more technical support specialists are needed to field their complaints. Third, technological advances hit the marketplace in the form of a new processor or software application so quickly that quality assurance departments cannot possibly identify all the glitches in programming beforehand. Finally, given the great variety of computer equipment and software on the market, it is often difficult for users to reach a high proficiency level with each individual program. When they experience problems, often due to their own errors, users call on technical support to help them. The goal of many computer companies is to release a product for sale that requires no technical support so that the technical support department has nothing to do. Given the speed of development, however, this is not likely to occur anytime soon. Until it does, there will be a strong demand for technical support specialists.

The Job

It is relatively rare today to find a business that does not rely on computers for at least something. Some use them heavily and in many areas: daily operations, like employee time clocks; monthly projects, like payroll and sales accounting; and major reengineering of fundamental business procedures, like form automation in government agencies, insurance companies, and banks. Once employees get used to performing their work on computers, they soon can barely remember how they ever got along without them. As more companies become increasingly reliant on computers, it becomes increasingly critical that they function properly all the time. Any computer downtime can be extremely expensive, in terms of work left undone and sales not made, for example. When employees experience problems with their computer system, they call technical support for help. Technical support specialists investigate and resolve problems in computer functioning.

Technical support can generally be broken up into at least three distinct areas, although these distinctions vary greatly with the nature, size, and scope of the company. The three most prevalent areas are user support, technical support, and microcomputer support. Most technical support specialists perform some combination of the tasks explained below.

The jobs of technical support specialists vary according to whom they assist and what they fix. Some specialists help private users exclusively; others are on call to a major corporate buyer. Some work with computer hardware and software, while others help with printer, modem, and fax problems. *User support specialists,* also known as *help desk specialists,* work directly with users who call when they experience problems. The support specialist listens carefully to the user's explanation of the precise nature of the problem and the commands entered that seem to have caused it. Some companies have developed complex software that allows the support specialist to enter a description of the problem and wait for the computer to provide suggestions about what the user should do.

The initial goal is to isolate the source of the problem. If user error is the culprit, the technical support specialist explains procedures related to the program in question, whether it is a graphics, database, word processing, or printing program. If the problem seems to lie in the hardware or software, the specialist asks the user to enter certain commands in order to see if the computer makes the appropriate response. If it does not, the support specialist is closer to isolating the cause. The support specialist consults supervisors, programmers, and others in order to outline the cause and possible solutions.

Some technical support specialists who work for computer companies are mainly involved with solving problems whose cause has been determined to lie in the computer system's operating system, hardware, or software. They make exhaustive use of resources, such as colleagues or books, and try to solve the problem through a variety of methods, including program modifications and the replacement of certain hardware or software.

Technical support specialists employed in the information systems departments of large corporations do this kind of troubleshooting as well. They also oversee the daily operations of the various computer systems in the company. Sometimes they compare the system's work capacity to the actual daily workload in order to determine if upgrades are needed. In addition, they might help out other computer professionals in the company with modifying commercial software for their company's particular needs.

Microcomputer support specialists are responsible for preparing computers for delivery to a client, including installing the operating system and desired software. After the unit is installed at the customer's location, the support specialists might help train users on appropriate procedures and answer any questions they have. They help diagnose problems as they arise, transferring major concerns to other technical support specialists.

All technical support work must be well documented. Support specialists write detailed technical reports on every problem they work on. They try to tie together different problems on the same software so programmers can make adjustments that address all of them. Record keeping is crucial because designers, programmers, and engineers use technical support reports to revise current products and improve future ones. Some support specialists help write training manuals. They are often required to read trade magazines and company newsletters in order to keep up-to-date on their products and the field in general.

Requirements

High School

A high school diploma is a minimum requirement for technical support specialists. Any technical courses you can take—such as computer science, schematic drawing, or electronics—can help you develop the logical and analytical thinking skills necessary to be successful in this field. Courses in math and science are also valuable for this reason. Since technical support specialists have to deal with both computer programmers on the one hand and computer users who may not know anything about computers on the other, you should take English and speech classes to improve your communications skills, both verbal and written.

Postsecondary Training

Technical support is a field as old as computer technology itself, so it might seem odd that postsecondary programs in this field are not more common or standardized. The reason behind this situation is relatively simple—formal education curricula cannot keep up with the changes, nor can they provide specific training on individual products. Some large corporations might consider educational background, both as a way to weed out applicants and to ensure a certain level of proficiency. Most major computer companies, however, look for energetic individuals who demonstrate a willingness and ability to learn new things quickly and who have general computer knowledge. These employers count on training new support specialists themselves.

Individuals interested in pursuing a job in this field should first determine what area of technical support appeals to them the most and then honestly assess their experience and knowledge. Large corporations often prefer to hire people with an associate's degree and some experience. They may also be impressed with commercial certification in a computer field, such as networking. However, if they are hiring from within the company, they will probably weigh experience more heavily than education when making a final decision.

Employed individuals looking for a career change may want to commit to a program of self-study in order to become qualified for technical support positions. Many computer professionals learn a lot of what they know by playing around on computers, reading trade magazines, and talking with computer professionals. Self-taught individuals should learn how to effectively demonstrate knowledge and proficiency on the job or during an interview. Besides self-training, employed individuals should investigate the tuition reimbursement programs offered by their companies.

High school students with no experience should seriously consider earning an associate's degree in a computer-related technology. The degree shows the prospective employer that the applicant has attained a certain level of proficiency with computers and has the intellectual ability to learn technical processes, a promising sign for success on the job.

There are many computer technology programs that lead to an associate's degree. A specialization in PC support and administration is certainly applicable to technical support. Most computer professionals eventually need to go back to school to earn a bachelor's degree in order to keep themselves competitive in the job market and prepare themselves for promotion to other computer fields.

Other Requirements

Technical support specialists should be patient, enjoy the challenges of problem solving, and think logically. They should work well under stress and demonstrate effective communication skills. Working in a field that changes rapidly, they should be naturally curious and enthusiastic about learning new technologies as they are developed.

Exploring

If you are interested in becoming a technical support specialist, you should try to organize a career day with an employed technical support specialist. Local computer repair shops that offer technical support service might be good places to look. Otherwise, you should contact major corporations, computer companies, and even the central office of your school system.

If you are interested in any computer field, you should start working and playing on computers as much as possible; many working computer professionals became computer hobbyists at a very young age. You can surf the Internet, read computer magazines, and join school or community computer clubs.

You might also attend a computer technology course at a local technical/vocational school. This would give you hands-on exposure to typical technical support training. In addition, if you experience problems with your own hardware or software, you should call technical support and pay close attention to how the support specialist handles the call and ask as many questions as the specialist has time to answer.

Employers

Technical support specialists work for computer hardware and software companies as well as in the information systems departments of large corporations and government agencies.

Starting Out

Most technical support positions are considered entry level. They are found mainly in computer companies and large corporations. Individuals interested in obtaining a job in this field should scan the classified ads for openings in local businesses. You may want to work with an employment agency for help finding out about opportunities. Since many job openings are publicized by word of mouth, it is also very important to speak with as many working computer professionals as possible. They tend to be aware of job openings before anyone else and may be able to offer a recommendation to the hiring committee at their workplaces.

If students of computer technology are seeking a position in technical support, they should work closely with their schools' placement offices. Many employers inform placement offices at nearby schools of openings before ads appear in the newspaper. In addition, placement office staffs are generally very helpful with resume and interviewing techniques.

If an employee wants to make a career change into technical support, he or she should contact the human resources department of the company or speak directly with appropriate management. In companies that are expanding their computing systems, it is often helpful for management to know that current employees would be interested in growing in a computer-related direction. They may even be willing to finance additional education.

Advancement

Technical support specialists who demonstrate leadership skills and a strong aptitude for the work may be promoted to supervisory positions within technical support departments. Supervisors are responsible for the more complicated problems that arise as well as for some administrative duties such as scheduling, interviewing, and job assignments.

Further promotion requires additional education. Some technical support specialists may become commercially certified in computer networking so that they can install, maintain, and repair computer networks. Others may prefer to pursue a bachelor's degree in computer science, either full time or part time. The range of careers available to college graduates is widely varied. *Software engineers* analyze industrial, business, and scientific problems and develop software programs to handle them effectively. *Quality assurance engineers* design automated quality assurance tests for new software applications. *Systems analysts* study the broad computing picture for a company or a group of companies in order to determine the best way to organize the computer systems.

There are limited opportunities for technical support specialists to be promoted into managerial positions. Doing so would require additional education in business but would probably also depend on the individual's advanced computer knowledge.

Earnings

Technical support specialist jobs are plentiful in areas where clusters of computer companies are located, such as northern California and Seattle, Washington. According to Robert Half International, Inc., the average technical support specialist earns between $25,000 and $36,500 a year. Those with more education, responsibility, and expertise have the potential to earn much more. Most technical support specialists work for companies that offer a full range of benefits, including health insurance, paid vacation, and sick leave. Smaller service or start-up companies may hire support specialists on a contractual basis.

Work Environment

Technical support specialists work in comfortable business environments. They generally work regular, 40-hour weeks. For certain products, however, they may be asked to work evenings or weekends or at least be on call during those times in case of emergencies. If they work for service companies, they may be required to travel to clients' sites and log overtime hours.

Technical support work can be stressful, since specialists often deal with frustrated users who may be difficult to work with. Communication problems with people less technically qualified may also be a source of frustration. Patience and understanding are essential to avoiding these problems.

Technical support specialists are expected to work quickly and efficiently and be able to perform under pressure. The ability to do this requires thorough technical expertise and keen analytical ability.

Outlook

The U.S. Department of Labor predicts that technical support specialists will be one of the fastest growing of all occupations through the year 2006. The U.S. Department of Labor forecasts huge growth—about 115 percent—of additional support jobs through the year 2006. Every time a new computer product is released on the market or another system is installed, there will unavoidably be problems, whether from user error or technical difficulty. Therefore, there will always be a need for technical support specialists to solve the problems. Since technology changes so rapidly, it is very important for these professionals to keep up-to-date on advances. They should read trade magazines, surf the Internet, and talk with colleagues in order to know what is happening on the cutting edge.

Since some companies stop offering technical support on old products or applications after a designated time, the key is to be technically flexible. This is important for another reason as well. While the industry as a whole will require more technical support specialists in the future, it may be the case that certain computer companies go out of business. It can be a volatile industry for start-ups or young companies dedicated to the development of one product. Technical support specialists interested in working for computer companies should therefore consider living in areas in which many such companies are clustered. In this way, it will be easier to find another job if necessary.

For More Information

For information about technical support careers, contact the following organizations:

The Association for Computing Machinery
One Astor Plaza
1515 Broadway
New York, NY 10036
Tel: 212-869-7440
Email: ACMHELP@acm.org
Web: http://www.acm.org

Webmasters

	School Subjects
Computer science Mathematics	
	Personal Skills
Communication/ideas Technical/scientific	
	Work Environment
Primarily indoors Primarily one location	
	Minimum Education Level
Some postsecondary training	
	Salary Range
$25,000 to $35,000 to $100,00	
	Certification or Licensing
Voluntary	
	Outlook
Faster than the average	

Overview

Webmasters design, implement, and maintain World Wide Web sites for corporations, educational institutions, not-for-profit organizations, government agencies, or other institutions. Webmasters should have working knowledge of network configurations, interface, graphic design, software development, business, writing, marketing, and project management. Because the function of a Webmaster encompasses so many different responsibilities, in a large organization, the position is often held by a team of individuals, rather than a single person.

The Job

Because the idea of designing and maintaining a Web site is relatively new, there is no complete, definitive job description for a Webmaster. Many of the job responsibilities depend upon the goals and needs of the particular organization. There are, however, some basic duties that are common to almost all Webmasters.

Webmasters, specifically *site managers,* first secure space on the Web for the site they aredeveloping. This is done by contracting with an Internet service provider. The provider serves as a sort of storage facility for the organization's online information, usually charging a set monthly fee for a specified amount of megabyte space. The Webmaster may also be responsible for establishing a URL (Uniform Resource Locator) for the Web site. The URL serves as the sites online "address," and must be registered with InterNIC, the Web URL registration service.

The Webmaster is responsible for developing the actual Web site for his or her organization. In some cases, this may involve actually writing the text content of the pages. More commonly, however, the Webmaster is given the text to be used, and is merely responsible for programming it in such a way that it can be displayed on a Web page. In larger companies Webmasters specialize in content, adaptation, and presentation of data.

In order for text to be displayed on a Web page, it must be formatted using *HyperText Markup Language* (HTML). HTML is a system of coding text so that the computer that is "reading" it knows how to display it. For example, text could be coded to be a certain size or color or to be italicized or boldface. Paragraphs, line breaks, alignment, and margins are other examples of text attributes that must be coded in HTML.

Although it is less and less common, some Webmasters code text manually by actually typing the various commands into the body of the text. This method is time-consuming, however, and mistakes are easily made. More often, Webmasters use a software program that automatically codes text. Some word processing programs, such as WordPerfect, even offer HTML options.

Along with coding the text, Webmasters must lay out the elements of the Web site in such a way that it is visually pleasing, well organized, and easily navigated. They may use various colors, background patterns, images, tables, or charts. These graphic elements can come from image files already on the Web, software clip art files, or images scanned into the computer with an electronic scanner. In some cases, when an organization is using the Web site to promote its product or service, the Webmaster may work with a marketing specialist or department to develop a page.

Some Web sites have several directories or "layers." That is, an organization may have several Web pages, organized in a sort of "tree," with its home page connected, via hypertext links, to other pages, which may in turn be linked to other pages. The Webmaster is responsible for organizing the pages in such a way that visitors can easily browse through them and find what they want. Such Webmasters are called *programmers* and *developers;* they are also responsible for creating Web tools and special Web functionality.

For Webmasters who work for organizations with several different Web sites, one responsibility may be making sure that the appearance of all the pages is the same (creating a "house style"). In large organizations, such as universities, where many different departments may be developing and maintaining their own pages, it is especially important that the Webmaster monitor these pages to ensure consistency and conformity to the organization's requirements. The Webmaster almost always has the final authority over the content and appearance of the organization's Web site. He or she must carefully edit, proofread, and check the appearance of every page.

Besides designing and setting up Web sites, most Webmasters are charged with maintaining and updating existing sites. Most sites contain information that changes regularly. Some change daily, or even hourly. Depending upon the employer and the type of Web site, Webmasters may spend a good deal of time updating and remodeling pages. They are also responsible for ensuring that hyperlinks within the Web site lead to the sites they should. Since it is common for links to change or become obsolete, the Webmaster usually performs a link check every few weeks.

Other job duties vary, depending upon the employer and the position. Most Webmasters are responsible for receiving and answering email messages from visitors to the organization's Web site. Some Webmasters keep logs and create reports on when and how often their pages are visited and by whom. Depending on the company, Web sites count anywhere from 300 to 1.4 billion visits, or "hits," a month. Some create and maintain order forms or on-line "shopping carts" that allow visitors to the Web site to purchase products or services. Some may train other employees on how to create or update Web pages. Finally, Webmasters may be responsible for developing and adhering to budgets for their departments.

Requirements

High School

High school students who are interested in becoming Webmasters should take as many computer science classes as they can. Mathematics classes are also helpful. Finally, because writing skills are important in this career, English classes are good choices.

Postsecondary Training

As of now, there is no set advanced educational path or requirement for becoming a Webmaster. While many have bachelor's degrees in computer science, liberal arts degrees, such as English, are not uncommon. There are also Webmasters who have degrees in engineering, mathematics, and marketing. Not all Webmasters have bachelor's degrees, however; some have two-year degrees, or a high school education only. Currently, most Webmasters do not have formal, specific training in how to design Web sites.

Certification or Licensing

There is strong debate within the industry regarding certification. Some, mostly corporate CEOs, favor certification. They view certification as a way to gauge an employee's skill and Web expertise. Others argue, however, that is nearly impossible to test knowledge of technology that is constantly changing and improving. Despite the split of opinion, Webmaster certification programs are available at many colleges, universities, and technical schools throughout the United States. Programs vary in length, anywhere from three weeks to nine months or more; topics covered include client/server technology, Web development, programs, and software and hardware. The International Webmasters Association also offers a voluntary certification program.

Should Webmasters be certified? Though it's currently not a prerequisite for employment, certification can only enhance a candidate's chance at landing a Webmaster position.

What most Webmasters have in common is a strong knowledge of computer technology. Most people who enter this field are already well versed in computer operating systems, programming languages, computer graphics, and Internet standards. When considering candidates for the position of Webmaster, employers usually require at least two years of experience with World Wide Web technologies. In some cases, employers require that candidates already have experience in designing and maintaining Web sites. It is, in fact, most common for someone to move into the position of Webmaster from another computer-related job in the same organization.

Other Requirements

Webmasters should be creative. It is important for a Web page to be well designed in order to attract attention. Good writing skills and an aptitude for marketing are also helpful for anyone considering a career in Web site design.

Exploring

One of the easiest ways to learn about what a Webmaster does is to spend time "surfing" on the World Wide Web. By examining a variety of Web sites to see how they look and operate, you can begin to get a feel for what goes into a home page.

An even better way to explore this career is to design your own personal Web page. Many Internet servers offer their users the option of designing and maintaining a personal Web page for a very low fee. A personal page can contain virtually anything that you want to include, from snapshots of friends to audio files of favorite music to hypertext links to other favorite sites.

Employers

Webmasters are employed by Web design companies, businesses, schools or universities, not-for-profit organizations, government agencies—in short, any organization that requires a presence on the World Wide Web. Webmasters may also work as freelancers or operate their own Web design businesses.

Starting Out

Most people become Webmasters by moving into the position from another computer-related position within the same company. Since most large organizations already use computers for various functions, they may employ a person or several people to serve as computer "specialists." If these organizations decide to develop their own Web sites, they frequently assign the task to one of these employees who is already experienced with the computer system. Often, the person who ultimately becomes an organization's Webmaster at first just takes on the job in addition to other, already-established duties.

Another way that individuals find jobs in this field is through on-line postings of job openings. Many companies post Webmaster position openings online because the candidates they hope to attract are very likely to use the Internet for a job search. Therefore, the prospective Webmaster should use the World Wide Web to check job-related newsgroups. He or she might also use a Web search engine to locate openings.

Advancement

Experienced Webmasters employed by a large organization may be able to advance to a supervisory position in which he or she directs the work of a team of Webmasters. Others might advance by starting their own business, designing Web sites on a contract basis for several clients, rather than working exclusively for one organization.

Opportunities for Webmasters of the future are endless due to the continuing development of online technology. As understanding and use of the World Wide Web increase, there may be new or expanded job duties for individuals with expertise in this field. People working today as Webmasters may be required in a few years to perform jobs that don't even exist yet.

Earnings

According to *U.S. News & World Report,* salaries for the position of Webmaster range from $50,000 to $100,000 per year. The demand for Webmasters is so great that some companies are offering stock options, sign-on bonuses and other perks in addition to salaries from $80,000 to $110,000. While this may be true for those who are hired into an organization specifically to fill the position, it is not representative of the many Webmasters who have merely moved into the position from another position within their companies or have taken on the task in addition to other duties. These employees are often paid approximately the same salary they were already making. According to the 1998 Webmaster Survey, the majority of Webmasters earn under $50,000. Nineteen percent of all Webmasters earned from \$25,000 to \$40,999 annually; seventeen percent earned less than \$25,000.

Depending upon the organization for which they work, Webmasters may receive benefits packages in addition to salary. A typical benefits package would include paid vacations and holidays, medical insurance, and perhaps a pension plan.

Work Environment

Although much of the Webmaster's day may be spent alone, it is nonetheless important that he or she be able to communicate and work well with others. Depending upon the organization, the Webmaster may have periodic meetings with graphic designers, marketing specialists, writers, or other professionals who have input into the Web site development. In many larger organizations, there is a team of Webmasters, rather than just one. Although each team member works alone on specific duties, the members may meet frequently to discuss and coordinate their activities.

Because technology changes so rapidly, this job is constantly evolving. Webmasters must spend time reading and learning about new developments in on-line communication. They may be continually working with new computer software or hardware. Their actual job responsibilities may even change, as the capabilities of both the organization and the World Wide Web expand. It is important that these employees be flexible and willing to learn and grow with the technology that drives their work.

Because they don't deal with the general public, most Webmasters are allowed to wear fairly casual attire and to work in a relaxed atmosphere. In most cases, the job calls for standard working hours, although there may be times when overtime is required.

Outlook

There can be no doubt that computer—and specifically online—technology will continue its rapid growth for the next several years. Likewise, then, the number of computer-related jobs, including that of Webmaster, should also increase. The World Organization of Webmasters projects an explosion of jobs available through the year 2006—well over 8 million. The majority of Webmasters working today are full-time employees—about 86 percent according to the 1998 Webmaster Study conducted by Collaborative Marketing. The newness of this job is reflected in the age demographics of Webmasters—35 percent are between the ages of 26 and 35 (1998 Webmaster Study); and according to *Web Week,* 72 percent are in their first Webmaster position. This indicates the attraction of the young to the Internet, and to better tap that market, a company's desire to fill Webmaster positions with young computer-savvy individuals.

The 1998 Webmaster Study found this field to be currently male-dominated. However, there is great opportunity for women. Many large companies, such as Wal-Mart, are looking for talented individuals who, according to a Wal-Mart Webmaster (yes, female) "can combine a lot of technical knowledge with the ability to cooperate with people who don't know a lot of technology. Women can often be very good at that."

As more and more businesses, not-for-profit organizations, educational institutions, and government agencies choose to "go online," the total number of Web sites will grow, as will the need for experts to design them. Companies are starting to view Web sites as more than a temporary experiment, but rather an important and necessary business and marketing tool. Growth will be largest with Internet content developers—Webmasters responsible for the information displayed on a Web site. The 1998 Webmaster Study predicts *Internet content developers* will become more sophisticated with their techniques and will significantly surpass the growth of the technical segment of Webmasters.

One thing to keep in mind, however, is that when technology advances extremely rapidly, it tends to make old methods of doing things obsolete. If current trends continue, the role of Webmaster will be carried out by a group or department instead of a single employee, in order to keep up with the demands of the position. It is possible that in the next few years, changes in technology will make the Web sites we are now familiar with a thing of the past. Another possibility is that, like desktop publishing, user-friendly software programs will make Web site design so easy and efficient that it no longer requires an "expert" to do it well. Webmasters who are concerned with job security should be willing to continue learning and using the very latest developments in technology, so that they are prepared to move into the future of online communication, whatever it may be.

For More Information

The Association of Internet Professionals represents the worldwide community of people employed in Internet-related fields.

Association of Internet Professionals (AIP)
9200 Sunset Boulevard, Suite 710
Los Angeles, CA 90069
Tel: 800-JOIN-AIP
Email: info@association.org
Web: http://www.association.org/index.html

For information on its newsletter, Webreference Update, and information regarding its voluntary certification program, contact:

International Webmasters Association
119 East. Union Street, Suite #E
Pasadena, California 91103
Tel: 626-449-3709
Web: http://www.iwanet.org

For information on education and certification, contact:

World Organization of Webmasters
9580 Oak Avenue Parkway, Suite 7-177
Folsom, CA 95630
Tel: 916-929-6557
Email: info@world-webmasters.org
Web: http://www.world-webmasters.org/

Index